Into Woods

Into Woods

Essays by

Bill Roorbach

University of Notre Dame Press

Notre Dame, Indiana

University of Notre Dame
Notre Dame, Indiana 46556
All Rights Reserved
http://www.undpress.nd.edu

Manufactured in the United States of America

Publication Acknowledgments
"My Life as a Move," *Roanoke Review* (spring 2002).
"You Have Given This Boy Life," *Crab Orchard Review* (spring 2002).
"Birthday," *River Teeth: A Journal of Nonfiction Narrative* 2.2
     (spring 2001): 55–72.
"Scioto Blues," *Missouri Review* 22:3 (winter 1999): 66–75, and
     excerpted as "Song of the Olentangy": *Harper's* 300.1799
     (April 2000): 34–37.
"Vortex," published as "Convocation," *Sport Literate* (summer 1999):
     17–24.
"Shitdiggers, Mudflats, and the Worm Men of Maine," *Creative Non-
     fiction* 9 (1998): 40–55.
"Honeymoon," *Columbia Magazine* 26.1 (spring 1996): 140–153.
"Into Woods," *Harper's Magazine* 286.1715 (April 1993): 75–80.

Library of Congress Cataloging-in-Publication Data

Roorbach, Bill.
     Into woods : essays / by Bill Roorbach.
     p. cm.
     ISBN 0-268-03162-2 (cloth : alk. paper)
     1. Roorbach, Bill. 2. Authors, American—20th century—
Biography. 3. English teachers—United States—Biography.
4. Outdoor life—United States. I. Title.
     PS3568.O6345 Z476 2002
     814'.54—dc21   2001006423

For Juliet

And for our parents:
Ursula and Frank, Reba and Jack

Contents

Into Woods

Honeymoon

In Paris the clerk at our three-star hotel gave Juliet and me a cheese-smelling second-floor room only a little wider than the bed. So we looked up the words for honeymoon and I went down to the front desk and grimaced and strung a few sentences together around that concept. A different clerk, a sour lady, grimaced too and said *all* the rooms were nice. So I changed from wanting a nicer room to wanting a higher room, a higher story for my *lune de miel*, and that impressed her. The new room was beautiful, with a balustrade window and a big bath and a desk.

Next day Juliet and I marched around in the ninety-nine percent humidity, trying out our French (I lack verbs, Juliet is fluent, but was rusty and shy) and nervous that in a restaurant they'd make us buy bottled water and serve us some mysterious, expensive organ we wouldn't want to eat, and glare at us and be famously rude, all of which happened. At least the Seine was there and flowed past (dead or alive) and at least, later in the afternoon, a stunning thunderstorm came and flooded the streets and cleared the air. We stood in a Latin Quarter doorway and watched the wakes of cars flush into the entrance of a clothing shop. The salesclerk just shrugged, took her shoes off, and waded around the store tidying the miniskirts and bathing suits on their hangers.

On the advice of married friends who said we should splurge shamelessly and without regret on our honeymoon, Jules and I rented a car. We followed a map and went out to the Atlantic Ocean for a few days. The air was cold, the water colder. The beaches were bleak and lined with hotels and empty cafes; you could see how crowded it would be in a few weeks. We made it south as far as the Île de Ré (which resembled our beloved Martha's Vineyard in that the locals abhorred summer dinks, and knew one when they saw one), then headed back inland to Cerqueux sous Passavant, where Juliet's art class would be. Cerqueux is a small town twenty miles south of Angers, an easy bicycle ride from Vihiers in the *département* of Maine-et-Loire, in the Anjou region. It's an agricultural village, with a miniature cathedral and a *boulangerie* and a cafe and a garage and a *mairie* and a bank branch and a post office.

The day we drove into town (July 1 of 1990), four thirteen-year-old girls sat on the steps of the church drinking from a bottle of Bailey's Irish Cream (of all possible choices!). They were quite drunk, but not hiding themselves, and no one seemed to care or even notice them. They went all polite when they heard our accents, said in embarrassed English that they didn't speak English, then in English said they didn't know where the *école* Albert DuFois was. We thanked them in embarrassed French, and everyone giggled.

We had paid the rent on a house, two hundred fifty dollars for July, but we didn't know where the house was, or what it looked like, only that it was on a wine farm within four miles of the school. We'd made a lot of jokes about this, pointing to wrecked barns and saying, "There's our house," or to châteaux and saying "That one." An old couple saw us sitting there in our car and pulled over, knowing that anyone who looked like us in that district must need help. They nodded wisely at Juliet's questioning, gave us directions to the Château des Landes. The château, when we found it, was decrepit and lovely, but the school wasn't there. The old couple had got confused because Albert DuFois had once owned the château (now broken into apartments). He'd also been the mayor of the town. "*Once* the school was here," a pleasant woman in the overgrown garden told us, in rather formal French. When we got back to Cerqueux, a charter bus was there, full of American art students.

The townspeople turned out for the bus, but the American artist who ran the school wasn't there. Everyone milled around, gradually realizing that he wouldn't be showing up, and that he'd left one of the townspeople in charge, though she was so quiet it was hard to tell. She pointed people into various cars. Many of the artists would be living with families, and the owners of these cars were to be their hosts. Those of us renting were matched up with landlords. I looked around hopefully, but no one seemed to take an interest in us. Juliet said her name, then said it louder.

"Oh, the newlyweds," the lady in charge said, with a great intake of breath. All the townspeople turned to regard us. "You will stay in Trémont. Les Moncellieres." Some of the women shook their heads in disapproval.

"I see none of the Rochelles have come to greet them!" a well-scrubbed woman said, patting at her apron.

A man introduced himself as the *boulanger*, the bread baker, and indicated that he'd see no great sacrifice in showing us to Les Moncellieres. "Perhaps the Rochelles are occupied and cannot come," he told us, cheerfully, in clear French.

An American student named Kellogg (this name writ large on her sweatshirt), fortyish, warm, and pleasingly fat, announced in English that she'd been here last year, knew the ropes, and would like to give us a hand. She and the *boulanger* shouted some simple French at each other, and between them figured out she'd be living not far from us. With no further excitement Kellogg hopped in the baker's truck, hollered at us to follow, and off they drove, very fast. We followed in our tiny Renault, past the church, past the last building in the village (which was a barn), past the cemetery (a wedge of walled earth beneath a large silver statue of the benevolent Mother of God), and through high farm country: rolling fields of wheat, tidy grape arbors, vast oceans of sunflowers, small fields of poor corn, shepherds' huts, woodlots.

We drove through another of the now familiar villages—red tile roofs, ancient church, shuttered houses. This was Trémont.

No stores, no cafe. A mile later the *boulanger* squealed into a driveway, passed two houses, and stopped in a dusty courtyard. He honked twice and leapt out of his truck. "Chez vous," he said, grinning. We were in the midst of a tumbledown farmstead, two houses and several huge sheds and many, many, small sheds and enormous stacks of hay and a tractor and an anomalously brand-new combine and two large gardens and twenty rotund cows in a high pasture behind the houses and barns. In the far distance several villages were visible on their ridges, cathedrals prominent. Grape arbors in dense rows covered all the hillsides, mile after mile. Next to us was a crude stone building with a sign, beautifully painted:

CAVEAU DEGUSTATION
Les Moncellieres

The *boulanger* grinned wider, embarrassed that no one was appearing. Clearly he was in a hurry. He said, "If you wait, they will come. I'm not sure where your quarters will be," then frowned, realizing we didn't want to be left alone.

"He's speaking French," Kellogg said helpfully.

The *boulanger* banged on the door of the second house, went back to his truck, honked his horn again. Then out of the garage of the first house—the bigger and prettier one—came an old man throwing his arms in the air, sputtering a welcome. His nose was purple as wine and shaped like a fist. "*Les Américains!*" he said. He was followed closely by an old woman, large and bent, who looked terribly embarrassed by her husband's ebullience.

"Louis Rochelle the elder," the *boulanger* said deprecatingly, by way of introduction. Louis regarded Juliet with robust pleasure, then looked skeptically at me.

His wife trundled up behind, examining me. "The newlyweds?" she whispered of the *boulanger*, who nodded.

Louis shook his head. "He is too old to be newly wed," he said. "Are you sure these are the newlyweds and not the wrong couple?"

"Yes," said the *boulanger*. He shrugged—what did he care?—we'd not be staying in his house.

Kellogg said a loud *bonjour* as Juliet showed Madame her new wedding ring, and lifted my hand too.

The old man shrugged, whispered, "One prays it is not a hoax." He raised his volume a couple of notches, said formally, "I am enchanted."

His wife loudly said something apologetic about her daughter-in-law, who was supposed to greet us, took Juliet's arm, and started back up the driveway between the gardens toward what she said was our house, a long, low building with a pair of French doors and two shuttered windows and two Dutch doors and a grapevine-covered shed for a garage, the whole thing clearly a converted outbuilding, charming. On either side of the French doors geraniums bloomed in large earthen pots. Juliet looked back at me, well pleased, and walked along with Madame. Kellogg swayed after. The *boulanger* threw his hands up and followed, too. I hovered back, to allow Monsieur Rochelle to join us, but he only winked, brought the thumb of his right hand to his lips, pinky in the air, then turned and ducked into the *caveau*.

At our place Madame Rochelle dug ten skeleton keys out of her apron, tried each three or four times, dug out ten more, finally unlocked the French doors, which opened wide into a big kitchen. She bid all of us wait, bustled inside to check the place, came back puffing with embarrassment, muttering once more about her miserable daughter-in-law. She bowed then, and Juliet entered. Kellogg followed, exclaiming in English how lucky. The *boulanger* wiped his finger on top of the refrigerator, raised his eyebrows at the tiny amount of dust.

Juliet dropped her book bag on the kitchen table, a vintage dinette set in steel and vinyl. The Virgin beamed down on us from a hutch full of odd dishes and utensils. And there was the *salle de bain* off the back of the kitchen, toilet in a separate room next to it, both with small windows to a spectacular view across the vineyards, the only windows in the back wall of the house, a hard breeze flying through. The parlor was dark, side by side with the bright kitchen, small window and Dutch door opening onto the garden, bright old paint, strips of leftover wallpaper, several nice patterns, cracked plaster showing horsehair. You felt dug into the earth, roots in a root cellar, safe and cool. The bedroom was the same, small window and Dutch door opening onto the glorious garden. Each room was furnished with a bed, big double frames stacked high with old mattresses, the stacks covered with worn purple-shag bedspreads from some lost phase of recent millinery history.

"The best we can do!" Madame blurted.

"But, it's magnificent," Juliet said.

Now Louis came up the driveway, drawing his sleeve across his mouth. We all stopped to watch him coming. Madame clacked her tongue, wouldn't let him in the house when he got there, stood barring the door. He paused on the cement stoop and took off his cap, ignoring her. "Newlyweds! Do you like the beds? Will two be sufficient? Do they have the proper resistance? Too soft and you'll never make connection!"

"I like the beds," I said, innocently, in my tentative French.

"Aren't they wonderful!" Kellogg said, robustly, in hers.

"Naughty man," Juliet said, joking, having understood Louis completely, as Kellogg and I had not.

The grinning *boulanger* checked his watch. We all strolled back to the cars, Juliet translating what had been said. At the courtyard Louis once again put thumb to mouth and pinky in the air. "A little taste?" he said.

"Ah!" the *boulanger* said, no longer in a hurry.

Madame sputtered, shook her head, made a face. "If you're going in there I shall go home and attend to the rabbits." She marched away.

"A bad marriage," Louis announced tragically, leading us into the cold breath of the stone *caveau*. A rusty refrigerator hummed. Next to it stood a homemade bar with two stools, which Louis bid us newlyweds take. Wooden barrels lined the walls. "It is here that we sell our wine," Louis said. "And back there that we make it." Through an old archway, stainless steel gleamed and a system of expensive-looking valves and glass piping climbed the wall. "The science is my son's, but he shall never make wine like mine!" Louis pulled two labelless bottles out of the refrigerator and uncorked them while Kellogg held forth in clear, loud French, thanking him.

After several glasses of the excellent wine, and a lot of stilted conversation, I seemed somehow to insult the *boulanger* by repeating the phrase *thou art the baker* over and over again.

All I was trying to do was to achieve an accent Juliet wouldn't laugh at. The baker sulked and glowered. Louis ignored him, came around from behind the bar, stood before Juliet. "I shall sing thee a song," he said. He puffed himself up, held out his arms and sang, formally, spiritedly, every verse and chorus of a long song, something about the birds of summer. His voice was pleasing enough, unwavering, proud. Kellogg and the *boulanger* listened passionately. Juliet stood frozen in embarrassment, the song directed straight into her face.

When he was done we all clapped. Louis looked lovingly into Juliet's eyes. "In a year thou shalt return with a baby!"

"A darling baby!" the *boulanger* cried.

"Nonsense," Jules said. She had just turned twenty-eight years old.

Later, the two of us sat at the kitchen table in our little house in candlelight touching hands across the table. "I feel like we've just gotten up from a horrible dream," she said. She meant our wedding, and the whole emotional year leading up to it, and the rush to the airport, and that rude hotel in Paris.

🍞

Juliet's classes took place at a farm called Bellevue. There the farmer had cleared out an enormous steel barn to make room for a makeshift *atelier*. The American artist had arranged for drawing tables and chairs. He'd installed two plywood model stands, upon which two American models would sit, naked. An old-fashioned realist portrait of Albert DuFois— painted by the American artist—hung next to the door. The *boulanger*'s wife sold croissants from a table in the courtyard (nothing too fresh since Americans weren't known to complain). Chickens poked around in a big pen near the house where Auguste, the farmer, took long lunches with his wife and neighbors and sons and daughters and rambunctious grandchildren, drinking gift whiskey and local wine with the loudest and most brash of the Americans, the ones who lived up to the stereotype and therefore most pleased him.

Juliet drew from the models in the mornings, came home for lunch and a two-hour siesta. We lolled in the sun of our porch or walked back to the grape arbors or napped in the cool of our room, the parlor, where we had thrown the best mattress on the floor. Then Juliet went back to the *atelier*, oil landscapes in the afternoon.

I worked at the kitchen table each morning from the time Jules left, sometimes turning to look out at the garden. Several frowzy rows of strawberries started it, running between the driveway and a wire clothesline strung on three rough poles. Charlotte, the daughter-in-law, loaded up the clothesline nearly every day at breakfast time with her sons' and husband's laundry, looking furtively at our door, hoping for any glimpse of what we might be up to.

On our side of the clothesline stood two sturdily staked rows of tomatoes, then yellow beans, radishes, shallots, carrots, garlic, onions, lettuce, cabbage. At the far right were six bushy rows of magnificent green beans, pressed up against the wall of the main barn. Four gnarled pear trees (Anjou!) at the back of the garden obstructed our view of the landlord's houses and his courtyard.

Every morning, about the time I'd got myself started for the day, *Grandpère* would slip through the pear trees, pad through the rows of garlic and materialize behind me at the kitchen doors, which I always left open to the breezes and the flies and the heat of the day. He'd feign respect for my solitude, say nothing till I turned around, then loudly: "Bonjour! Une petite gout?" Thumb in mouth, pinky in the air. He had the conviction that I was lonely, cuckold to Juliet's art, that my writing was a morbid hobby and not to be encouraged. He spoke slow, careful French, and took pains to be sure I'd understood whatever he'd said: "I am more sympathetic than the others here, for I too had to learn a foreign tongue, when I was a prisoner in Germany."

Every morning he was in one of the gardens, his job in forced retirement, raking potatoes, watering, weeding. If I caught his eye he'd shout out a hello, come marching over, gleeful: "Bonjour! Bonjour! How didst thou sleep? Was thy pecker nice and stiff? Thou found'st her unspoiled, one hopes! What's this? Writing again?"

"It's my work."

Thumb in mouth, pinky in the air, "A little taste?"

"No, I'm sorry, it's too early for me."

"With these Americans it's always 'sorry'!"

"Well, thank you, but I'd be sleepy. I wouldn't be able to work anymore."

"But it is thy honeymoon! No work for thee till thy wife returns! How without wine will thy cornstalk grow?"

"Grandpère, Juliet and I have been lovers eight years!"

He spat and shuffled off to drink alone.

The Rochelles were three generations: *Grandpère* and *Grandmère;* Louis *Petit,* their son; his ample wife, Charlotte; and their three boys, the grandsons, Antony, Pierre, and Hubert. Hubert was much younger than the other boys, was the darling of his mother and grandparents, had the freedom of the place. Antony and Pierre at fifteen and seventeen were farmers already, on a strict schedule of work, manning the tractors each morning at eight, driving off to spray and clip the vines or spread manure or to plant cabbage between rows of new vines or to harvest the wheat or bale the hay. Their father, Louis *Petit,* would saunter out of the house around nine, never earlier, gaze over at our house to see what I was up to, only then hop in his little truck and be gone. I waved to him every day for a week before I met him. Some days he waved back. He was the only farmer I've ever seen who wore shorts on the job, every day, tiny blue shorts tucked up under his big firm belly. His wife did the paperwork and all of the cooking and the laundry, and worked in the garden, their grocery. They all of them were wary, seemed to think we spent our time making plots against them in league with *Grandpère.* What was I so jolly about, after all, and what did we say to each other in English?

Grandmère brought over green beans or plums or eggs or onions or lettuce, convinced we were starving to death. *Grandpère* brought shallots: "Good for the penis!" Charlotte rather begrudgingly, even suspiciously, told Juliet we could use her washer and clothesline, as if she thought my underwear would be two stories high, or otherwise disreputable. Juliet gave them all drawings, which they adored. They loved beautiful Juliet. It was I who remained the problem!

✍

Evenings we newlyweds made good dinners with the bountiful local ingredients, or ate at Les Routiers, the chain truckstop on the Saumur road (a splendid place with long tables and cheap seven-course dinners and free wine and sensitive French truckers in groups), or found some of the artists in town and had parties. In the cool of the night we looked at the stars a long time, watched the owl who lived in the grapevine draped over our car shed, watched the bats beeping at insects, then closed up the French doors and were alone. In the morning the roosters crowed, and not long after that *Grandmère* came into the garden, brought us eggs.

If the grandparents had us over for wine, the daughter-in-law wanted to know what they'd said. If we had dinner at Louis *Petit*'s (which we did only once: a soft-core porno film playing on the TV throughout, jiggling boobs, men's tightened buttocks, burned steaks and plenty of garden produce), *Grandmère* wanted to hear how bad it was. If *Grandpère* gave me a bottle of wine, Louis *Petit* gave me two. If Charlotte gave us six plums, *Grandmère* gave us every cherry from their yellow cherry tree.

The Rochelle grandsons seemed always to take offense at me, old codger that I was, but they were very solicitous of Juliet. Antony was the first to call, one early evening, bearing a bottle of red wine. "For you," he said in tortured English. "This wine." In French he said that it was from his father's stock, and none of that lousy stuff his grandfather made. "Your name?" He got my name quickly enough, "Like the *Buffalo Beel*, n'est ce pas?" but Juliet's took more doing. When he got it, he blushed, brightly, looked at her as though he would swoon: Shakespeare! He himself was named thus!

Many evenings young Antony found a reason to visit, his hair wet and combed, his thin self dressed in a fresh shirt. He brought Juliet a radio, since she had said she missed music. He brought her a bottle of wine. They'd chat in hip French, or a little in English, so he could practice. I tried making jokes in my stilted, formal French, but Antony was still wary of me. I learned too slowly not to smile or to laugh or to try to joke in front of him, or anyone, until he or they knew me. But Antony kept coming back. He loved Juliet's drawings. He liked her long hair, and said so frequently, asked to see her brush it. He gazed frankly at her long legs in her all-American cutoff shorts, all but stroked them for her, all but kissed them. His Gallic eyes burned. A movie star, right here on his family's farm! To hell with her bodyguard!

Antony's dad, Louis *Petit*, called me into the *caveau* one afternoon, took me through the maze of his wine operation, which beneath the cracked roof tiles and behind the ancient walls was quite modern and complex. His specialty as listed in the wine books was Rose d'Anjou, but his best-seller locally was a good hearty red, sweet and spicy. He also made a white wine, which he admitted was terrible, but which he said was popular amongst a certain clientele, ladies from Vihiers. From a 1,000-liter, stainless-steel tank he poured red wine into glasses whose stems had broken off, walked me back into the musty *caveau*.

I attempted a complicated pleasantry, something about the mix of modern and ancient elements in his operation.

"So," he boomed, saying each word clearly so that I would not fail to understand. "You think that farmers are ridiculous?"

"Why no," I told him haltingly, "not at all, my own uncle is a farmer."

"I suppose his farm is much bigger than this, and his cattle fatter?"

"Why no, not at all. In fact, his farm is small and quite poor."

"But bakers, I suppose you find bakers ridiculous?"

"Why no, not at all! Why do you say that?"

"Your French isn't so good, you know."

"I make, I think, I hurt, I insult, I make the baker?"

"You are impossible to understand." He went back and poured us more wine, stood before me with his chest thrust out in manly challenge.

"I like it here," I said.

"Who comes to a farm for his vacation?"

"It is my honeymoon."

"My honeymoon, too, was on this farm. I worked each day of it, and could not say which day it was over. How old are you?"

"Thirty-six."

"Well, I am thirty-seven." The way he said it made it mean everything he wanted it to mean, nasty things about Americans who thought they were better than bakers and farmers, soft, childless, teacher types who pretended to write, who rented cars in Paris and blotted the landscape doing nothing useful, nothing at all for an entire month in the most important season of the year.

"I will be thirty-seven in August," I said, an inadequate answer, but all I could come up with.

"Do you expect a drink because of this?" He puffed his chest out again, not happy that I was bigger than he, not happy that I was American, not happy with me at all. Finally—and suddenly—he smiled, just at the moment the air got too thick to breathe. He poured us more wine, lifted his broken glass. "To the new husband," he said.

On weekends, with the art school closed, Juliet and I made day trips. Often we drove to Saumur, eighteen miles away. We sat by the Loire and watched the fishermen dapping with sixteen-foot poles. We ate crêpes in the square, hiked up the many stairs to the château—whole, handsome, and high on a limestone bluff over the town and the river, its four towers and deep walls commanding a view up and down the valley, the Loire like a sliver of sky parting the earth, spanned by medieval bridges. We drove to see ruined castles at Chinon and Martigné-Briand and Passavant and Beaufort, stopped at *pâtisseries* and little bars and food shops, stopped anywhere that had a sign, or a place to sit. I played with my wedding ring, pulling it off and dropping it often, fishing it out of cracks in sidewalks or the upholstery of chairs. Juliet turned to cut her eyes at me whenever she heard its distinctive *ping*. I had never before worn a ring of any kind. It made my left hand look like my father's left hand, pinched my finger, meant nothing as a symbol, nothing I thought it might: our love was greater than any statement jewelry might make!

And we went to Angers for art supplies and books and maps, visited museums and monasteries and the ruins of abbeys and limestone caves and sacked cathedrals on the way. The best was the cathedral of Doué-la-Fontaine: no roof, no interior walls, no guards, no gates. We entered through a thirty-foot high window, thought about all the years of the world. In Tigné, the next village north of Trémont, part of a Roman aqueduct stood in the middle of a farmstead, filled with millennia of dirt, growing poppies. The farmer was a shouting prick, and his dogs were nasty, too; one could only view the ruin from the road, and only briefly, once the dogs got wind. Near our house were several modest châteaux (most smaller than the average suburban house in Greenwich, say, or Grosse Pointe), outfitted with moats and turrets. Windmills were everywhere, none working, some reduced to conical stone bases with goats on top, or grapevines.

At a sweet little bakery in Tigné we bought most of our bread, insulting the *boulanger* from Cerqueux further. In Vihiers, the nearest large town, we shopped sometimes in an American-style grocery store, the Super U, until we discovered the Wednesday morning *marché*, merchants who moved together from town to town throughout Anjou, joining local farmers. Each Wednesday morning, spread out across the Vihiers town square and running into side streets, a hundred booths sprouted, much junk for sale—purses, t-shirts, baskets, hardware—but also food: eggplants, onions, goat cheese, sausage, cold cuts, seafood, dove's eggs, cow's tongues, cake. And living things, too: chickens stuffed in sacks, chicks in long boxes, ducks held by the feet, snails still crawling, rabbits in baskets or lofted by the ears.

We saw complete castles at Brissac and Vihiers and Champigny and Langeias and Montsoreau, all of them smaller than I'd expected, not the grand castles of the eastern Loire, but awesome still, and open. At what I'll call Tigné-LeClerq the lady of the house, the actual Countess Tigné-LeClerq, gave us a tour of the castle that was still her home; she preferred not to, she said, but had to give tours to receive government restoration monies, which were significant. She was tall and erect and really very elegant, used French words unapologetically whenever her English failed her. The tour was all business: famous stone carvings, castle keep, working drawbridge, spectacular vaulted cellars, but nothing of the living quarters, no furnished rooms at all, nothing of the soul of the place.

Juliet kept up an appreciative conversation, one countess to the other (clear French to the countess's clear English), which is the way, in some string of sentences I missed, that our hostess learned we were newlyweds. She softened. She cooed. She found herself very fond of Juliet, eyed me with rather less suspicion than I'd grown accustomed to, actually took Juliet's hand, asked her all about growing up in New York City. She knew Central Park West, certainly, where Juliet's parents still lived. She knew several people at the Metropolitan Museum, across the park. She knew the village too, and Soho, and deigned to hear about the funky loft I had lived in with friends and no heat and motorcycles and grand piano, my own sort of castle. And suddenly through a massive door we were in her *home*, the part of the castle she'd kept private. She showed us her kitchen—enormous, part medieval, two solemn cooks at work in chef's hats—showed us her living room—intimate, all modern, uniformed maid standing by—showed us her gallery— dark paintings in great gilt frames. We stared and stared at those paintings, two portraits, four landscapes, a still life.

The countess put her chin in hand then, considering, finally brought us up a tight stone stairway to a spotless tower bed chamber with a view through open stone windows (gossamer curtains blowing), a grand view across the fields to the Loire and beyond, another big castle in sight over there (Montreuil-Bellay, she said), round bed in satin sheets, nightstands carved of stone, thick candles, chamber pot, water pitcher, fireplace the size of our bathroom back in New York (our own apartment certainly not on Central Park West!), fire laid unlit.

"You must stay," said the countess in English.

"But we are too poor," Juliet said in French, gasping.

"My gift," said the countess.

One hot August morning at Les Moncellieres, as I sat ruminating at the kitchen table, sneezing in the haytime dust, I heard conversation behind me in the garden. I focussed in slowly on the French, began to hear it, but even then it took several sentences to realize that *Grandmère* and Charlotte were talking about me. "Look at the beer lover just sitting there." This was Charlotte, speaking rapidly in her querulous mumble, increasingly easy for me to understand. "He says he writes," *Grandmère* said.

"To me it appears he is sitting," Charlotte replied, unimpressed.

"Well, don't forget, he is newly wed."

"Have you seen? He's put their bed on the floor!"

I turned and waved, showed them my pencil, my pad of paper, turned and went back to work.

"Having a fine nap?" the daughter-in-law said brightly.

"How is your vacation?" *Grandmère* said.

And Charlotte: "I hear you like castles better than farms!"

The women worked daily like this for an hour or two, right behind me, their great bottoms in the air, filling baskets with weeds or with produce, sporadically chatting, clearly not fond of each other, but pleased to have a subject for gossip so close to hand.

Now *Grandpère* came, waddling up the driveway behind his olden wheelbarrow. In it was a twenty-liter wine jug, one of his son's deposit containers for local customers, quite full, the purple of the wine showing through the white plastic. He stopped abruptly when he saw that the women were in the big garden, turned his wheelbarrow behind a plum tree and set to work in the smaller garden across the drive (two rows of artichokes in bloom forming a tall purple stripe between ten rows of potatoes and ten rows of cabbage). After a while he'd pulled enough weeds to hide the side of the wine vessel that would be toward the women, so proceeded, wheeled his barrow to my door. "Bonjour!" he called, ignoring Charlotte and *Grandmère*.

"Your American is having a fine nap," Charlotte told him.

"He's only tired," *Grandmère* said generously.

"I'm writing," I said, but my accent hadn't fully awakened yet and they couldn't understand me. This reinforced their firm belief that I couldn't understand them.

"Look at him, just sitting there, plucking at his nose hairs!"

"Be glad he paid the rent!" *Grandpère* called, wheeling his wine and weeds to the potato *caveau*, a shed attached to the very far end of our long house. He disappeared inside for a moment, reappeared with the wheelbarrow empty. He made much of rolling the garden hose, ended up with it neatly at my door. I kept at my writing pad, scratching, scratching, trying to ignore his presence, which was like a warm and itchy wool blanket around me. Finally I turned.

Louis grinned, sidling toward the potato cellar, thumb to mouth, pinky in the air. I joined him—what the hell!—I joined him, drinking glasses of wine in the near-dark next to two big piles of potatoes, discussing the beauty of a hoe handle he'd carved, feeling its smoothness. *Grandpère* had a few words to say too about the absolute inevitability of my fatherhood. One glass of wine, two, and not even eleven o'clock yet. Three glasses, four, the two of us grinning complicitously. Finally the old man declared it time to go back to work. He pounded me a fond pat on my back, walked me to my door, wheeled his barrow on, steadily. The women, thank goodness, were gone.

In my kitchen I put my head on my pad of paper and slept the morning away. Just before Jules got home I heard Charlotte's sneering voice from the garden: "You see? Sound asleep!" When I turned, Charlotte was there with a little crowd—*Grandmère*, Louis *Petit*, Antony, and Hubert. They all of them had come to see for themselves.

Afternoons at the *atelier* the artists spread out around Bellevue to paint landscapes near enough the *atelier* for the arthritic (and very appealing, I should say, and talented) American artist to find them and give advice and instruction. Bellevue lived up to its name, not in the sense of being a mental hospital, but in offering good vistas on all sides, distant farms, shapely trees, new-mown hay in round bales receding to the horizon, windmills, ponds, cathedral spires—distance and light and space; color and shadow and depth. Juliet set herself up in front of a field of sunflowers, hectares of cheerfully drunken yellow faces bobbing in the breezes. I dropped her off at the *atelier* most afternoons and stayed twenty minutes, strolling around the farmstead looking at the various artists' interpretations, good and bad, chatting with Kellogg and the other friends we'd made.

The American artist had a house in town, had conceived of this school as a way to pay for living there. The little house was part of a street-front row of houses, an ancient place in much need of repair whose windows looked out on the fallen houses around it. He'd painted all the interior walls with classical subjects: Autumn as a woman whose breasts spilled out over her bodice, Summer as a dancing nymph, paintings that made me think unaccountably of Juliet's and my tower room in the castle Tigné-LeClerq. His parlor was a gallery, and people came from all over Anjou to buy paintings from him. The townspeople, in turn, nearly all of them, had thought of ways to make money from the American artist's students. It was a cozy, symbiotic system.

On a Saturday, brioche day, I went down to Cerqueux and tried to make up with the baker, explained that I hadn't meant to insult him, that it was only my lousy French.

"So," he said, "You prefer the bread from Tigné?"

Jules and I went to Saumur for the fourteenth of July. Several thousand people had gathered on the banks of the Loire and on the medieval bridge that spanned it. At something imprecisely near eleven o'clock all the town lights went off, everything, a blackout, all the streetlights, all the restaurant neon, all the auto lights, all the lights in homes. Jules and I sat quietly on the southern bank of the Loire in blackness. For five minutes all was hushed and dark, just the river coursing past, deep and quiet. Then a rocket went up, just one, a stream of orange sparks, then a silent explosion and a sparkling like sunlight on water. More fireworks went up, one or two at a time for an hour. The rockets rose progressively higher as the show continued until finally a bright orange stream went high enough that its flower burst directly over the castle as the full moon rose behind.

⟋

Louis the Elder took me for an evening tour of his vines. He was worried why Juliet wasn't home, didn't think that an evening model session at the *atelier* was an adequate story. He kept shrugging, sweetly, concerned for me, and pointed out the vines that he owned, those that his son owned, those that his evil neighbor owned. "These with the thick stalks were planted by my father just before the war. These over here I planted just after. One can see that mine are superior. My father—that old dog whom no one remembers kindly—was the first to graft American vines onto French roots, at least here in Trémont. This prevented the spread of disease. Those over there, 1965. Quite strong, as one can see. The white powder is for mildew. They say the powder won't kill a person, but I don't believe that!" To give me the words for *graft* and *mildew* he repeated them over and over, pointing at the graft lumps at the bases of his vines, sniffing with his nose at imagined mildew. He meant for me to understand every word he said, made me rephrase everything to prove I had it right. "These vines are getting too old, here, but the wine is my favorite, so I save this section for myself. It's ideal growing weather here, all of the year round, but the soil is terrible. Thou hast seen the fools trying to grow corn? Louis *Petit* tried it two years. Phut. With all his machines. And he buys more and more land, more and more grapes, more and more tanks to store wine so he may sell when the price is high. More and more and more! Bigger and bigger and bigger! What is wrong with stability? Constancy? Satisfaction? It's as if he's trying to be an American, always growing, growing till he's too big and falls from the weight!"

We walked down the rows of grapes, turning from one arbor to the next, until we had turned so many times I became confused. I was surprised when I saw the barn and realized we were nearly back at the farmstead. Louis put his thumb hopefully to his lips, his pinky in the air. I nodded, followed him to the *caveau*. We filled our glasses from one of Louis *Petit's* 1000-

liter tanks and drained off two glasses of wine each, then three. "To my son, the ungrateful prick, and to my bad marriage and to his."

We drank. Louis waxed misty. "There were snakes in Anjou when I was a boy. Big snakes as thick as thy penis. *Salut!* But people didn't like the snakes, and now they are killed and gone. Nothing is wild here. Everything is planted. Everything managed. A deer walks by like a pet, and is shot in his season. A rabbit is the son of the son of an escaped meal! The fish in the pond? I put them there. The fish in the Loire? The government puts them there. Only the storms are wild anymore! Only the hailstones! Only the wind, drying everything!" He drank. "To thy new little baby. Thou must name him *French!*" He said *French* in English, the only word of English I ever heard him use. "May there be snakes everywhere he travels, and may strong winds knock him down, again and again, again and again!"

Our honeymoon proceeded. No day was much different from another. The church bells tolled at the same hours, the weather was hot and clear with a strong western breeze. The sun set in our bathroom windows at ten, the nights were cool and long. The boys came out of their house at eight and got on their tractors and trundled away; Louis *Petit* came out at nine, stared over at me, got in his little truck and drove off; Charlotte hung the wash; little Hubert raced through the garden, scared to death I'd say hello. And *Grandmère* came and picked tomatoes, or weeded, or sprayed water with the hose; *Grandpère* came and asked me to join him for a taste of wine. I walked the farm some afternoons, or swam in the pond, or rode Antony's bicycle, searching the countryside for Roman ruins.

And each evening sweet, complicated Juliet came home from the *atelier* and we ate—fresh foods plain and exotic from the outdoor market, tomatoes from the garden, bread from the *boulanger*, wine from *Grandpère*—then watched the long sunset, slipping late back into our house, which was simple and no castle tower, simple and cool and cozy and our own, lit our candles, closed the French doors and were alone.

Into Woods

In a dive near Stockbridge in the Berkshire Hills of Massachusetts, I nearly got clobbered by a big drunk who thought he'd detected an office fairy in the midst of the wild workingman's bar. He'd heard me talking to Mary Ann, the bartender, and I didn't talk right, so by way of a joke he said loudly to himself and to a pal and to the bar in general, "Who's this little fox? From Tanglewood or something?"

I, too, was drunk and said, "I am a plumber, more or less." I was thirty years old, was neither little nor a fox, had just come to work on the restoration of an inn, and was the foreman of the crew. More or less. But that seemed like the wrong answer, and too long in any case.

He snorted and said to everyone, "A more or less plumber," then appraised me further: "I say a hairdresser."

"I say a bank teller," his pal said.

I didn't mind being called a hairdresser, but a bank teller! Oh, I was drunk and so continued the conversation, smiling just enough to take the edge off. "Ah, fuck off."

"Cursing!" my tormentor cried, making fun of me. "Do they let you say swears at the girls' school?"

"Headmaster," someone said, nodding.

"French teacher," someone else.

"*Guys. . . ,*" Mary Ann said, smelling a rumble.

"Plumber," I said.

"More or less," someone added.

"How'd you get your hands so clean?" my tormentor said.

"Lily water," someone said, coining a phrase.

My hands? They hadn't looked at my hands! I was very drunk, come to think of it, and so took it all good-naturedly, just riding the wave of conversation, knowing I wouldn't get punched out if I played it right, friendly and sardonic and nasty all at once. "My hands?"

My chief interlocutor showed me his palms, right in my face. "Work," he said, meaning that's where all the calluses and blackened creases and bent fingers and scars and scabs and cracks and general blackness and grime had come from.

I flipped my palms up too. He took my hands like a palm reader might, like your date in seventh grade might, almost tenderly, and looked closely: calluses and scabs and scars and darkened creases and an uncleanable blackness and grime. Nothing to rival his, but real.

"Hey," he said. "Buy you a beer?"

My dad worked for Mobil Oil, took the train into New York every day early-early, before we five kids were up, got home at six-thirty every evening. We had dinner with him, then maybe some roughhousing before he went to bed at eight-thirty. Most Saturdays, and most Sundays after church, he worked around the house, and I mean he *worked*.

And the way to be with him if you wanted to be with him at all was to work beside him. He would put on a flannel shirt and old pants, and we'd paint the house or clean the gutters or mow the lawn or build a new walk or cut trees or turn the garden under or rake the leaves or construct a cold frame or make shelves or shovel snow or wash the driveway (*we washed the fucking driveway!*) or make a new bedroom or build a stone wall or install dimmers for the den lights or move the oil tank for no good reason or wire a 220 plug for the new dryer or put a sink in the basement for Mom or make picture frames or . . . Jesus, you name it.

And my playtime was an imitation of that work. I loved tree forts, had about six around our two acres in Connecticut, one of them a major one, a two-story eyesore on the hill behind the house, built in three trees, triangular in all aspects. (When all her kids were long gone, spread all over the country, my mother had a chainsaw guy cut the whole mess down, trees and all.) I built cities in the sandbox, beautiful cities with sewers and churches and schools and houses and citizens and soldiers and *war!* And *floods!* And attacks by *giants!* I had a toolbox, too, a little red thing with kid-sized tools.

And in one of the eight or nine toolboxes I now affect there is a stubby green screwdriver that I remember clearly as being from that first red toolbox. And a miniature hacksaw (extremely handy) with "Billy" scratched on the handle, something I'd forgotten until one of my colleagues on the Berkshires restoration pointed it out one day, having borrowed the little thing to reach into an impossible space in one of the eaves. Billy. Lily.

My father called me Willy when we worked and at no other time. His hands were big and rough and wide, blue with bulgy veins. He could have been a workman easy if he wanted, and I knew it and told my friends so.

⌇

In my rich suburban high school in Connecticut we were nearly all of us college track, which meant you could take only two shop classes in your career there.

First half of freshman year you could elect Industrial Arts, which was an overview: a month of Woods, a month of Metals, a month of Technical Drawing. Second semester, if you still wanted more, you went into Woods I, Metals I, etc. I loved Woods. I loved hanging out with some of the rougher Italian kids, Tony DiCrescenzo and Bobby LaMotta and Tony Famigliani, all of them proud and pleased to be tracked away from college. I wanted to hang out with Tommy Lincoln and Vernon Porter and Roland Fish, the three black kids in my class, all of them quietly (maybe even secretly) tracked away from college. Wood shop was first period, and it was a wild class. Mr. Schtenck, our little alcoholic teacher, made no effort to control us and often left the shop for the entire period to sit in his car.

The rough kids used the finishing room to smoke pot, the storage room to snort coke. We all made bookshelves and workbenches and record racks and knickknack shelves and lamps and tables and guitar stands and frames for photos of our girls. The year was 1968, so we also made elaborate bongs and stash boxes and chillums and hollowed-out canes and chests with secret drawers. Wood shop (and along with it the very act of working with my hands) took on a counter-cultural glow, the warm aura of sedition, rebellion, independence, grace. Sophomore year I signed up for Woods II, which was the advanced course. My guidance counselor, Miss Sanderson (a nice enough lady, very well-meaning, very empathetic—you could make her cry over your troubles every time if you played your cards right), thought I'd made an error on the electives form. "Only one elective a semester, William. Surely you'd like a writing course! Journalism! Or how about Occult Literature?"

"Woods II," I said, flipping my hair. I had to get parental permission to take Woods again and thought a little note with my mother's neat signature would be easy to snag, but it was not. "Why do you have to reinvent the wheel?" Mom said, one of her phrases, something of a non sequitur in this case, her meaning being *someone else will build the furniture.* Her next question was, "What kind of kids are in that class?"

Dumb kids, Mom. Mostly Italian kids and blacks and, of course, Alvin Dubronski (the class moron) and Jack Johnsen (the plumber's kid!) and me. My dad thought it was fine, especially with the alternative being literature courses where who knew what kind of left-wing occult hippie doubletalk Mrs. Morrisey would tell you!

So into the wood shop again, every day first period (if I wasn't late for school; by that time I was hitchhiking to avoid the uncool school bus). I was the only college-track kid taking Woods II, maybe the only college-track kid who had *ever* taken Woods II, though the other kids got to take it semester after semester. And I got peer-pressured into smoking pot in the finishing room and occasionally even into blowing coke in the storage room, always a sweet, nerve-jangling prelude to another round of boring college-track classes.

One day when I was in the storage room with my high-pressure peers (and the two smartest kids in Woods II, maybe in school, both destined by their blackness for bad times in Vietnam) Roland and Tommy, fat Tony Famigliani stuck his head in the door: "The Stench is coming!" But Schtenck was already there, standing in the door. I saw my college-track life pass before my eyes.

"What are you little fuckers doing?"

"We're tasting coke, sir," Tommy said, the idiot, total honesty, as we'd all learned in Boy Scouts.

Florid Schtenck raised his eyebrows clear off his face, said, "Jesus Christ, boys, put it away—you want to get me *canned?*"

He never looked in the storage room again.

And later that year he stumbled and cut his finger off on the band saw. For two weeks then we had a substitute who made us file all our plans and actually checked them, stood beside us as we drilled holes in our wood or turned bowls on the lathes. It seemed an eternity before Schtenck came back and we could finally fill all the bong and hash-pipe and stash-box orders we'd been sitting on. *Sedition.* The next year I took Woods II again, having secured special permission from the principal to go along with my parents' special permission and the special permission from Miss Sanderson. Senior year I signed up for the class once more—what the hell—but I don't think I ever got to school in time to attend.

✑

Somewhere in there I stopped being a willing volunteer for my father's list of chores. Now he had to *command* me to help with his corny weekend projects. I had better things to do, things in the woods with Linda or cruising-in-the-car things with some of the guys in my various garage bands—minor-league dope runs into Greenwich Village or actual gigs in actual bars in Port Chester, where the drinking age was eighteen and we could get away with it.

At home things were quiet. Except for my long hair, you wouldn't have noticed that a teen was testing his folks. I was good at talking to my elders, and good at hooking grades without working too hard—college track—and very, very good at staying out of trouble. I was on the student council. I helped with the student newspaper. I went to the homecoming rallies and proms and parades. I memorized the headlight patterns of the town police cars (I still get nervous around those big old Plymouth Furys), could smell a cop from miles away, leagues away, light-years. I had a plan for every eventuality and an escape route from every party.

Weeknights I'd turn in early, out to my room over the garage, wait for the main house to quiet down, then slip out into the night. I was caught only once, coming home about five in the morning with a friend named Bonita. Someone had called me after I'd left, and Dad couldn't find me. He was asleep in my bed when Bonita and I walked in. I was grounded, and here was the punishment: I had to spend the next four Saturdays and Sundays helping him build a playroom in the basement, drilling holes in the concrete for hours to anchor the plates for a gypsum board wall, running cable for a hanging light over the bumper-pool table, slamming up paneling, churlishly working side by side with my dad and his distinctive smell, Old Spice mixed with cigarettes and Head & Shoulders and sweat.

✐

The college track barely got me to college. As part of my desultory rebellion I put off applying until well past all the deadlines, never lying to my folks, never lying to my guidance counselor, but showing all of them the forms ready to go, then just plain old not mailing them. My plan was to play rock and roll and maybe—if necessary—make money working as a carpenter, or maybe drilling holes in concrete, or maybe making furniture or bongs. Then Miss Sanderson got a list of our school's applicants from one of my supposed top choices, and I wasn't on it. Crisis! April already, when most kids were hearing from Colby and Yale and Michigan and the University of Hawaii.

My trusty guidance counselor got on the phone and found some schools that would look at a late application. She was crushed for me, so crushed she spared my parents the full brunt of my dereliction. At hastily arranged late interviews, admissions counselors never failed to ask why I'd taken Woods II *six semesters straight*. Finally I was accepted by one famously lame school, to which I resigned myself; then, at the last possible minute and by great good fortune, I was put on the waiting list at Ithaca College, where, on August 21, one week before school started, I was admitted into the freshman class.

I never saw my father at work, and he never talked about his work, which I vaguely knew was Executive and had to do with Mobil Oil and was desky and involved meetings and much world travel and made us pretty rich. And because I'd never seen him at work, my natural adolescent impulse toward emulation had little to go on. What to imitate? How to surpass, destroy? What I saw of my valiant dad was his work around the house, and so, emulation gone awry, I set out to be a better home handyman than he'd ever be, the real thing, even, a tradesman.

Two dollars and fifty cents an hour was well known as great money, nearly double what I'd made stocking frozen foods at the A&P during high school. Two-fifty an hour was what truck drivers got, longshoremen, a full hundred rasbuckniks (my father's word) a week. I dropped out of Ithaca College in my junior year (just when most of my buddies were heading off for a year abroad), went back to Connecticut (not my hometown, God forbid, but one nearby), and went to work for an electrician.

Lawrence Berner was a former electrical engineer who'd thrown it all over at age sixty, a theory ace but a fairly clumsy worker, a guy who had actually tossed away everything and left the college track for good. Larry was British and Jewish and unconventional and very charming, all qualities that impressed me. Best of all, he was divorced, the first divorced person I'd ever seen up close. He was filthy of habit—decadent, disgusting (maybe not as bad as my friends at school, but Larry was *old*). He lived in his marital house, wife long gone, and had trashed the place, filled the garage with electrician junk, filled the kitchen with dirty pots and jars and cans and dishes, filled the refrigerator with his important papers (fireproof, he said), filled the bedroom with the most slathery skin magazines imaginable, filled the whole house with take-out cartons, TV-dinner tins, and his own filthy underwear. His living room seemed buried in death.

He paid me $2.50 an hour. Working beside him (tradesmen often touch—four hands to pull the cable, four arms reaching into a small space, heads together to look into a service panel . . . *hey, hold my legs while I lean out over this here abyss*), I'd feel sometimes like I was with my dad. It was Larry's thin hair, maybe, or the Old Spice and cigarettes, or just regular old transference. I spent every day beside this parallel-universe effigy of my father, and I was mad at Larry almost always and desperate to impress him.

One day he said I had good hands, and that little compliment was everything—I glowed, I crowed, I told my friends, my folks. I stared at my hands late at night in bars, stared at them for hours, entranced. And my hands got callused, grotesquely callused, were always covered in cuts and scratches and dings and scabs that I hardly felt. Your knuckles never healed. And Larry mostly worked *hot*, meaning with the power on, because it saved time. I got shocks and blew holes in screwdrivers. I hit my head on rafters and slammed my thumb with hammers and fell off ladders and sliced my fingers (daily) and once even poked a screwdriver hard into my eye (the blade didn't penetrate the eyeball but rolled past it and into the socket so that old Larry had to pull it out . . . and we kept on working). I drove the truck sometimes, sweet-talked the customers, ate in diners, worked squinting with a Lucky Strike in my mouth, no filter. I put in panel boxes and wired 200-amp services and installed a thousand outlets and a million switches. I drilled holes for cable, sawed rafters, snaked wire through walls. I wriggled into crawl spaces, sweated in attics, dug trenches for UF cable.

I liked it. All that body work. But, like every college-track kid in America, I'd been taught that someone else would do the rough stuff if I'd just use my mind. And the sense that there was some higher calling nagged at me, the sense that all I'd heard about college was right. So after a year and a summer of the trades, I went back to Ithaca, pleasing my parents enormously, no surprise. The surprise was in how happy I was. Suddenly I was a great student—all *A*s, excellent attendance, papers handed in on time—fully engaged in a tough fight against the possibility of being a tradesman, the possibility of taking Woods II for *life*.

But after the college track had run its course, I needed to make money. I failed tests for newspaper jobs (*twenty minutes: neatly type a 500-word story around the following facts . . .*), gagged at the thought of ad agencies ("We keep you clean in Muscatine," to quote a line from F. Scott Fitzgerald's first gig out of Princeton), moved around the country for a long time (coast to coast, north to south), worked with cattle (rode horses, too), bartended (which left your hands clean, at least, and put you in the path of women), played music in the most local of local bands, finally landed age about twenty-eight in a friend's loft in New York City, state of New York, where I kept up the music in better bands and great clubs, but to no great rewards, in fact, penury. Bartending jobs were sought after, thus impossible to get. Corporate writing jobs beckoned: public relations, newsletter editor, copywriter, hack. I even answered an ad for someone to write porno. At least I knew something about *that*. "Adult novels," the ad in the *Village Voice* said. Turned out to be a mill, and the job was to type a minimum of a book a week *directly into the typesetting machine!* Dollar a page, one hundred sixty page books, one-sixty a week a fortune. Torrid love engines, mossy grottoes. Better than lying about pollution controls or profits for bigger companies. On the subway out to Queens I changed my mind, pulled off my tie (a *tie*—who did I think was going to interview me?), untucked my shirt, changed trains at the next stop, rode back to Manhattan, broke.

I got the bright idea to put up posters around the Village and Soho and Tribeca and be a handyman. Independence! And the amazing thing is, it worked. Calls came in immediately—did I know how hard it was to find someone to do small jobs? People would hear my estimates and laugh, offer *more*. I did every sort of odd job for every sort of odd person, moving over the months and years to larger home repairs, bigger prices, leaving town to restore that Berkshires inn, coming back to sub myself out to contractors. I graduated finally to a specialization in kitchen remodels and new bathrooms, getting more and more deeply into the role, hiring helpers, wearing my one suit to estimates, taking tiny but unbelievably productive ads in fancy magazines (well, *New York Magazine*), cracking the codes for admittance to the wholesale supply houses, getting good at all of it, twelve years total, Woods II, until one day I woke up and realized I was about to take out a bank loan to buy a truck and some very expensive tools, about to start looking for a storefront, about to start paying my ragtag musician employees *on the books*.

I headed straight to grad school.

Juliet and I spent lots of our free time last summer looking for a house to buy here in Farmington (my apprentice tenure-track teaching job, a year out of Columbia, a year after our wedding—a dreamy year we'd spent in Montana—was at the University of Maine branch campus here). It would be our first house. An old farmstead, we hoped. I kept telling myself that I had an advantage, which was my haphazard twenty-year fund of construction knowledge and restoration experience. I looked up at the beams and poked at the foundations and lifted the vinyl siding and pulled away carpets. I wiggled toilets and pulled on pipes and pushed on all the walls and ceilings. I got in crawl spaces and pried open hatch doors, inspected wiring, eyeballed plumbing, made the real-estate folks happy: they love a guy who thinks he knows what he's doing.

And sometimes, in light of this commitment, this buying a house on a small piece of our little planet, I thought about what would happen if the legislature shut down my branch of the University of Maine, or what would happen if I didn't get tenure, or what would happen if I just couldn't take the bureaucracy anymore and quit. Well, not to worry. Education presidents come and go, but people always need a plumber or someone to fix the roof. Or renovate inns. I could take my clean college hands and plunge them into work, open all the old scars, stop being mincy and fastidious, once more revel in goo and slime, get into it—wrestle cable, kick at shovels, stand in the mud all day, hook my leg around ladders in the wind, lay tile, lift toilets and plunge my hand down that reeking fuzzy hole to pull the clog (poor Raggedy Andy one time, usually worse).

Juliet and I found a house, bought it, moved in. And immediately my dad, now retired, came up to visit, tools in hand. The two of us got up early the first morning he was here and headed out to the garage, a forlorn little outbuilding about to fall down and stuffed to the rafters with the owner-before-last's junk (mostly pieces of Volkswagens and cans of old bolts and misshapen gaskets and used spark plugs and odd shims and clips). My plan was to leave room to park a car, sure, but to build a wood shop, a work space from which to operate while Jules and I renovated the house (a neglected nineteenth-century "quarter-cape" with many additions, the newest of which is a porch built in 1953, my own year).

So for hours my dad and I worked. We cleared out and sorted all the junk, ripped down the cardboard that made the walls, stopped to stare, to think, came up with opposite plans, argued, convinced each other, switched sides, argued again. Finally we jacked up the north side of the garage, replaced the sill, dropped a corner post in cement, took the jack away, rebuilt the wall. Next we shored up the south side, added wiring, installed a metal roof over the leaky old asphalt shingles. We hit our heads and cut our fingers and ripped our jackets. We peed in the woodpile. We argued, mostly about technique and a little about the Education President, that first George Bush (who was about to go), but really, I guess, about who was in charge of the work in my garage. And even though Pop was helping me for free, even buying some of the materials, I fumed and fulminated, sulked, complained, reverted to a painful adolescence.

Still, we rebuilt the barn-style sliding door and cut in a window. We ate companionably in the Farmington Diner with sawdust and plain dirt in our hair and new hammer holsters on our belts (the acerbic Yankee waitress looked me over, said, "Hi, Professor," and I introduced her to my dad); we went to the dump; we gabbed at the lumberyard; we swung hammers, climbed ladders, cut wood; we gazed at our work a long time in the dark when we were done.

Pop said, "You saved that building," as if I'd done it on my own, and we went on in the house to wash up.

Spirits

Right away our new neighbor Lulu Lawrence came over to greet us with a pie and a booklet (this written by a local lawyer in 1969) giving the history of our new neighborhood and showing a grainy photo of each house on our new road. From the photo Juliet and I learned that our enormous new elm had not changed much in twenty-three years—good news, as it is one of the few healthy old American elms left in Maine or in the world. We also saw that our sagging new porch had been plumb and true back in that summer of moonwalks and Woodstock and, for me, a Montana idyll, complete with church-camp girlfriend, only the fear of conscription into a lingering war to darken bright days.

Under the photo of our new house—I photocopied the page and have it here in front of me—this:

MRS. MARY BUTTERFIELD FOLSOM'S HOMESTEAD
(*Present owners: the Thomas C. Moonrobins*)

When Isaac Butterfield, Jr.'s daughter, Mary, married W. F. Folsom in 1874, they built this place on a part of the old Butterfield farm on the south side of the road leading from West Farmington to Temple. It was about opposite her father's place.

Mary's husband and infant son died within three years after her marriage. Isaac, Jr.'s house burned at about the same time, so Isaac and his wife, Phebe, moved into the Folsom home. Mary soon went to work at the "Little Blue" School, and later she married Thomas A. Stevens and moved from this home. One of Mary and Thomas Stevens' children, Mrs. Nora Allen, who is still living in Farmington, supplied us with much of the information in this booklet regarding the Russell's Mills neighborhood.

In 1878, Isaac Weston Butterfield, only son of Isaac, Jr. and Phebe, married Fannie Stevens. Isaac W. and his bride then settled on the farm with his parents.

In 1882, shortly before his death, Isaac, Jr. deeded all his property, which included this place, to his wife, Phebe. Seven years later she deeded the place to Frank A. Thompson, minor son of Phebe's daughter, Ellen, who had married Albert Thompson in 1869. Frank deeded to Albert Thompson in 1937, and Albert sold to the Henry J. Manns in 1951. Subsequent owners were the Frank Lindsays, Jacob Wirth, the Harold Beaches, and in 1956 the present owners, the Thomas C. Moonrobins bought the place.

Along the way, each owner had added on. The original building is tiny, a "quarter cape," our likeable real estate man called it (with exaggerated respect), a local architectural term that a builder friend tells me really means half a cape—Cape Cod house, that is. A number of quarter capes were built in these parts by thrifty do-it-yourselfers using a widely sold, colonial-era blueprint for a whole cape. This blueprint people of limited means simply halved, like a recipe. This half-a-house contains our living room and narrow foyer-stairwell downstairs, and one bedroom with steep eaves upstairs, a bit of an attic above that, nothing more. The basement beneath is lined with fieldstone, and is wet in spring: mud floor.

Before 1900, an unknown one of the owners named above built an addition southwards, a large el, as such additions are called in Maine, making room downstairs for what would eventually be Juliet's studio and our bathroom, upstairs for an unfinished attic, which, after a lot of work, now daunting, may one day be our master bedroom. The next addition grew eastwards, another el, long and thin, containing our parlor with its seven doors and woodstove and our dining area downstairs, and the eccentric eaves rooms, two in a row with different level floors, that would make our guest room and my office (where I sat as I first typed this bit of parenthetical nonsense), soon enough to become a kid's room, one hoped. From the far end of this el, one of our antecedent owners attached yet another el, this one heading southwards again, making of the whole house a bit of a wacky horseshoe. South of this blunt el, which is wholly our kitchen, our predecessor Frank A. Thompson—no earlier than 1911—built a barn. I know that date of limitation because doing repairs I found dated religious broadsheets used as the vapor barrier between the clapboard siding and the sheathing. *Jesus calls you unto him as sheep unto his fold.*

At the back of the barn was fastened a two-seat outhouse poised over a grown-in stony vault. Gravity had pulled so long with the aid of weather that the structure was hanging from its own bent and naked nails, some of them the old cut-nails, some newer wire-nail additions, all letting go. So, a couple of years into our ownership, I put a crowbar at the top of the thing and boom it fell to the lawn. I was sad about its loss, turned out, and still am a little mad at myself—but at the time it seemed crazy to spend a month renovating an outhouse. I kept the board with the two holes cut out. That will be a sign one day: *Lentior!* Which will translate as the name of our house: Slow Down.

I put daylilies in the pit and have used some of the beautifully heavy old outhouse boards around the house for various projects, including repairs under our substantial porch, which I didn't want falling as the outhouse had done, and did save.

Thomas Q. Moonrobin added the porch, Lu Lawrence told me. And Moonrobin added the cinderblock foundation that stopped the eastern end of the house from its sinking. (A ball dropped by one of our dogs rolls forty feet from the westward living room and through the parlor to the eastward dining room *fast*. The walk from the kitchen to the living room is not just slanted but strongly *uphill*. This, I love.) "Moonrobin was a charactah," Lu said. She would hate me for spelling it like that, but that's how she said it. "His wife died in your house," said Lu. "He raised four kids here," she said. "He was a lovable, yuh, generous, hardworking man, yuh- yuh- yuh." She shook her head, looked skyward, lost herself in reverie.

When she came back to our shared world, she told me that Moonrobin had built all the outbuildings, too, the odd little structures that had sold me on the place. She wondered what had become of him. He'd been the mailman on this route—Rural Route Four—thirty years or more. "A sweetie, he was," Lulu told me. "When Annie died, oh he folded in, yuh! Left his job," Lu said, "He almost did die himself." Then the ultimate expression of empathy, breathed inward: "Yuh. Yuh. Yuh!" She paused, collected herself. "Got dark and closed off and wouldn't talk."

Moonrobin sold to a California Couple (they're still called California Couple in the neighborhood, no name remembered), who sold it quickly to Pete and Marnie Johnson, who sold it in turn to us—Bill and Juliet (the Professor and the Artist, I know people call us, and I know the tone)—with improved gardens, septic system, and other landscaping, sold it to us in 1992 after some mild negotiation for the sweet sum of $48,500.

And the Professor and the Artist lived in this house year-round for four unimaginably speedy years before the Professor changed jobs (trading rugged landscape and beloved home for a more rugged career landscape, for cruel ambition) and the Artist went off to school in Chicago, eventually joining her husband in plain Ohio, proving their permanent and unarguable status in Maine as Flatlanders.

The Moonrobin place became our summer house. And though we held onto the idea that we would be back someday, back full-time, we were certifiable Summer People, which, of course, is not good (the only even slightly acceptable Flatlander is a year-round Flatlander). But oh! Our blessed, blessed summer place! It wasn't so hard to afford: our mortgage is $369.12 a month. In winter, a good-natured, super-handy bachelor with his own summer plans housesat for us, paid the bills on the basis of shut-off notices, kept the grounds gorgeous. Our plans fit his plans, it seemed, and he kept coming back.

✐

We started with a couple of acres that were sectioned off in 1951 when Albert Thompson got sick of the family house (our house, that is, still called the Thompson place by many of our neighbors, the ones who don't call it the Moonrobin place) and put up a deluxe double-wide mobile home across the street and two hundred yards down the hill and out of sight.

A couple of years into our tenancy, Lu Lawrence (who with her late husband bought her house, the former Little Blue School, from Thompson), decided to move to senior housing in town. She came over and made a rather formal speech: as her abutter (pronounced abuttah), I had every right to first refusal on the woods between her place and mine. So Juliet and I now own four more acres, a beaver-bitten and stone-wall woodlot that touches the Temple Stream: nine thousand bucks. I thought it a good deal—still do—but certain towns-folk smirked.

The rest of the old Butterfield farm—hundreds of acres—was still a milk farm, owned by Dennis Lucky, then not yet forty, bought (as he has told me) from his former employer. The pastures were still clear; the Temple Stream still ran through the flood plain below; the heifers still gamboled; the steers still mooned, the bull still thought he reigned; the cows still chewed and stared and bellowed giving birth, still came up the hill for milking; the birds were still plentiful and various: stream, field and forest habitats converge here and with luck always will—Dennis has lately moved up Porter Hill a mile and wisely put his streamside land into conservancy.

On our land, the rusting hulks of two '30s Ford coupes still hunker in the brush by the stonewall under apple trees, hunker there along with a considerably newer VW bug body. A third old car was towed out of there by a gentleman who said he "Couldn't help but notice." Couldn't help but notice an old hulk rusting under mounds of vines out of sight of the road? And then there was the wringer-washer, a Kenmore, an artifact too, but too bright white and too glaringly visible under the vines. This I apologetically escorted to the Farmington dump, which has, by the way, the best view from any dump in New England, and is now a transfer station only.

Dear old Mrs. Thompson across the street has since passed away, but when we moved in, that spry old surveillance expert still lived across the street from us in the aforementioned double-wide. Juliet and I threw a neighborhood party our first spring (no one would have come before we gained resident-alien status by lasting through the winter), and Mrs. T drove her Subaru wagon 150 yards to come see us. She stayed barely long enough to say our cheese tasted funny and to tell us she had lived in our house just after her wedding. Oh! we said, thrilled, and the other guests gathered around, ready for a charming tale.

"I always hated this place," she croaked. "Awful, awful place! Drafty! *Drafty!* Water in the basement, rats in the roof, those brittle locust trees always crashing down, dandelions, *pink* clover—you still have *pink* clover in the lawn."

Up the hill and spread through the Temple Stream valley are several Thompsons descended from Frank A. Thompson and his brothers, Thompsons everywhere, in various-size houses and various apparent levels of wealth. One meets them in the neighborhood, good people all.

But Moonrobin. Tom Moonrobin was gone from the neighborhood, and his name with him. I knew that odd name before we even moved into the house from folks around who, when I told them exactly which house I'd bought, would shake their heads fondly and say "The old Moonrobin place." (That if they didn't shake their heads dismissively and say "The old Thompson place.") And always the person would add a warning: "I hear that place is sinking," or "That place has a cracked foundation," or "That porch Moonrobin built will have to come down," or "You bought yourself a project, yes-you-did, yuh."

Oh, a project indeed. My buyer's remorse was mighty in the days after we moved in. But our yard fell away to the south and was bathed in sun and the trees were beautiful—October light—and we owned them. Our first land, our first house. It didn't take a week for the flaws to recede and for pure puppy love to commence. I stood out in the untravelled road at night and just gazed at our house: *Is a very, very, very nice house.* I dreamed up all the remodeling projects and yard projects that are finished now—by my hand, by Juliet's, with my father's help and that of friends and well-paid helpers: windows repaired, everything repainted, new bathroom, new kitchen, new plumbing, new electric, new basement stairs. Stop me or I'll go on. Stop me or I'll list the next ten years' worth.

But what I loved most at first were the ramshackle outbuildings, three of them pressed right against the west property line, forming something of a barrier between Dennis's overgrown barnyard and our undergrown lawn (yes, full of pink clover, dandelions, too, and a dozen other plants that take to mowing, some resembling grass). Lowest on the south-running hill was a little hut that we thought might eventually be a guest house or writing studio. We kept stuff in there that we couldn't quite yet part with—old chairs, broken fishing rods, dented filing cabinet, six bags of hardened mortar mix, one rotting suitcase. Before us the little building was the Johnson girls' playhouse. In fact, it was the darling sight of those girls in there playing cards around a child-size table that sold me on the Moonrobin place. It was as if I were peering into the future, seeing those children there.

After we moved in, we found notes written in the very smallest corners of the eaves on the wallpaper in our bedroom. We cut them out when we remodeled—still have them, little squares of ancient wallpaper, elegant girlish handwriting:

> Missy Johnson.
> September 30, 1992.
> Lived it and loved it.

> Tina Johnson.
> September 30, 1992.
> Lived it and loved it too.

In this hut were twenty sugaring pails and a muscular old Glenwood woodstove too big to hug, tall as a sixth grader, squat as a fireplug but purpose opposite.

Slightly uphill from the playhouse and toward the road was a tenuous, sprawling shack held up by cedar trunks and framed in scrap wood. Add some corrugated sheet metal and old window sashes, tie the whole thing together with cables and turnbuckles and more nails than you'd believe (try getting a board off the wall!). A great place to stand in the rain, big open doorway, raindrops drumming on tin. My dad named this one the Shack, and it's attached to the old garage he and I restored into a shop. He named the lowest building the Sugar House, naming so we could communicate. Where's the hammer? Shed? Shop? Shack? Sugar House?

That garage was the first project. We'd need a good shop, a place to cut wood, to repair window sashes, to make dust, to make a mess, to splash paint, to keep the house itself as livable as possible as much as possible. Trouble was, when you put your hand on the leeward wall the whole garage swayed a foot to the northwest. You'd walk to the other side and push and it would sway a foot back to the southeast, stopping only when the cable (heavy linesman's cable that someone with a taste for the halfway had strung from the northwest eave to a leaning box-elder tree) went taut—*sproing*—went taut and caught the building from falling. Inside was junk. I'd begged the Johnsons not to worry about all that—to leave it. Mr. Thomas C. Moonrobin had left it for the California Couple after all, and the California Couple had left it for the Johnsons. But I, unlike those other Moonrobin successors, have uses for junk. I love junk. And if anything had impressed me more than the sweet little girls playing cards in the Sugar House—loving and living it—it was the sight of all that tumbled junk, that rusting stuff, that collection of manufactured castoffs so crowded that you could hardly pick out individual items, so dense that you could not enter the garage.

First day in, October 1, 1992, I marched around the yard a dozen times, halting for the view of our four hills and Mount Blue not far distant. I inspected each tree, walked the stone walls, found grapes, found raspberry bushes, found apples. Birds, birds everywhere. I admired the garden plot, the single pumpkin left behind. I inspected the car bodies, the dump-bound old washing machine. Behind the stone wall I found the base of an old boiler, found a witch's cauldron, dragged them up to the lawn, stacked them, made a sculpture. My heart filled, my remorse fled, the sun beat down. I looked in the play-house, looked in the barn—junk everywhere—checked out the storage shack. I fought my way into the garage, started picking through the debris Moonrobin had left. No one had disturbed any of it.

First clue: a set of vintage dog tags, complete with chain. Moonrobin, Thomas Q. His serial number. His rank: PFC 4. I began to sort, heaving anything rotted or rusted or broken or otherwise useless straight out the big sliding garage door into the back of my truck: leather horse traces, blacksmith's apron, worm-growing medium, World War II vintage jeep windshield, rusted steel bucket filled with rusted HO-scale traintracks, portional roof antennae, seventy small plastic jars with red tops in a single grocery bag, rolls of kraft paper, wet.

After a long afternoon of work I got to the workbench, an astonishingly oily setup made of old two-by-twelves, ten feet long, much chopped and gashed and beaten and gouged—hand of the worker made visible—hand of the child, too: a hundred headless nails protruded and many screws and three broken-off drill bits. The workbench was piled high with more and more and more detritus. In coffee cans were gaskets from various engine types. To the dump. Hanging from hooks were more gaskets from even more engine types. To the dump. Cans of screws. Keep. Boxes of recycled nails. To the dump. Jars of bolts. Keep. Envelopes of instructions for long-gone appliances and tools. To the dump.

There were toolboxes, some of them just fine. In one was the missing sprayer from our kitchen faucet set, never installed (but it would be). In another, more gaskets, lots more gaskets, gaskets for every possible fitting on every year of VW bug back through time to the Stone Age. To the dump. But in a heavy old box I found a glorious assortment of rat-tail files, twenty files with no handles, all sharp, all as oily as a Texas well and thus preserved.

And calendars, keep. Calendars turned forever to specific months—the march of time: May 1955, the month my sister Carol was born; December 1960, the Christmas I got my red bike. On the back door into the shack: August 1969. Woodstock! My sixteenth birthday! Good omens. Keep, keep. There were license plates to predate the calendars, the oldest a Maine trailer license dated 1954. High on the wall, a burn-craft plaque, boxy letters:

Tom Moonrobin 1957

But the timbers and siding were all much older than that—this Moonrobin had built the place with used wood, perhaps from a garage that had predated this one.

And tacked to the wall over the workbench was a little cutout from the Lewiston newspaper which I have since lost, but will boldly paraphrase from memory:

Driver of VW spared in Train Collision

Kelly Moonrobin, 17, of Farmington, was spared when his Volkswagen sedan was hit by the Clark Mill train and crushed at the Anson Road crossing.

"She darn it stalled at the worst place you could think," said Mr. Moonrobin. The southbound lumber freight, according to police, hooked the VW's bumper and dragged the vehicle two hundred yards before a signal pole forced its fender under the locomotive, which was traveling all the while at approximately fifty miles per hour.

"It was a bad ride," said Moonrobin, who was miraculously unhurt, having been thrown clear of the wreckage.

"God has pity on drunks and fools," said Engineer Ernest Melton, of Peacham, Vermont, who was unable to halt his train more quickly. Mr. Moonrobin was cited for driving while under the influence of alcohol and was released into his father's care.

In the next toolbox was an empty fifth of Blunt's Gin, not the last I would find, not the last by many dozens. Father or son? To the dump. In the next, six oily box wrenches—useful. In the next—a big, dented workbox, very heavy, locked—something grand, I hoped: an hour looking for my hacksaw in all our packed U-Haul cartons still in the living room, five minutes sawing, and I'd found Moonrobin's archives: Every bill he'd paid in forty years, it seemed, mostly insurance on a succession of VW bugs, but insurance too on a Jeep, and later on a station wagon. Pension papers from the Army. Phone bills for four dollars, complete.

Somewhere in the middle of the pile I happened on the photo of a smiling young woman: really very pretty, hopeful and happy, ripe and plump. On the back in a looping hand:

Tom my secret, Tom my love.

Later I'd find a bottle of Hai Karate cologne, still some left, still fragrant, purposefully hidden in the eaves above the workbench. Father or son?

I kept digging. What had kept the floor from rotting out under the buckets of rain that got through the mossy roof was oil, lots of it—motor oil—leaked from the pans of a succession of VW bugs over the years, splashed during years of do-it-yourself repairs. Useless spare parts dominated my finds: three VW hubcaps spray-painted gold (those old moonies with the logo in the center), VW mudflaps, two rearview mirrors, a heater hose, a glove-compartment door, thermostats, carburetors, axle parts, u-joints, taillights, headlights, parking lights, horns. I could have built a bug.

Some of the stuff had nothing to do with cars: lots of woodstove parts, a cigar box containing exactly six guitar picks and a pocket knife, the temperature gauge from a sugaring boiler, a homemade ice-chopping tool, two street signs (JCT ROUTE 56, snaky curve icon), a fishing reel and part of a rod, a handkerchief, one pair of coveralls, two broken Christmas-tree stands, a violin bow, two boxes of books, a virtual encyclopedia of home repair. Also, much evidence of children: on the barn-style door (which depends from wheels that roll on a well-greased track) four names at four heights, spray painted in the handwriting of four different school ages: Kelly, Tim, Mark, Leslie. Humble Tom didn't go for juniors.

My neighbor Dennis Lucky stopped over to stare awhile, said he remembered when this garage held a rock band made of Moonrobin sons and the Thompson kid from up the hill. "Loud as hell," he said. "And bad." And he remembered when Mrs. Moonrobin died. He said he thought maybe, well you could never know, but just maybe, that's why Tom had moved. And yes, the Volkswagens, the many many Volkswagens, and the noise Kelly made working on them, the famous train accident.

I cleaned and organized and cleaned some more, made four trips to the dump, then rebuilt that garage with my dad's help—replaced the roof, shored up the walls, cut the cable that had held the poor building up these many years. And in some kind of gesture to the past I closed Tom Moonrobin's dog tags into the wall, just nailed them to a stud and covered them with insulation and drywall. And so they remain, hidden and benignly powerful, ticking in there like some telltale heart.

A couple of years passed. Everywhere, Moonrobin clues: a *Club* magazine from 1978, graphic snatch shots on cheap paper, unfaded, hidden in the knee wall of the attic room. Son, I'm guessing. Mason jars with collected bugs sealed inside and a Barbie slipper. Daughter. And, hell if I haven't found every possible sort of faulty amateur repair: one electric circuit with a heavy screw jammed where the fuse should have been accounted for *all the electric outlets and lights in the house*. The kitchen sink drained into the side yard rather than into the septic tank. A leaking valve buried in the *driveway* connected to a defunct water system. Thomas Q. Moonrobin. All fixed now.

And, you know, you dig a hole in the yard and find part of a fishing rod. You use a file and realize as you rasp away that it's Moonrobin's file. You finally get around to installing a sump pump in the little basement, and find everything you need—including the pump and fifty yards of black coiled p.v.c. pipe and clamps and electric bits—in pieces all around the house and grounds, all stuff too good to throw away, all collected decades back for a purpose. Moonrobin had meant to get around to the sump pump, too.

One fine weekday my third fall here, I was working in the yard, propping up the little oak trees that the Johnson girls had planted (these are thirty feet tall now—amazing growth), and up pulls a car. Oh, brother. Jehovah's Witnesses? The building inspector? Some former student? Another Republican hopeful in the wrong place? And a large man gets out. A very gentle, large man, you can see the gentleness from the first second in the way he carries himself, like a mail sack full of dainty, fragile figurines. He's apologetic in his every wiggle, hurries to me in my yard. He says, "Pete? Pete Johnson?"

"No," I say, carefully reserved, "But he lived here once."

"You bought from him!"

This, of course, is nobody's business. I just gaze at this man, liking him despite the interruption, and of course not realizing who he is.

"Tom Moonrobin!" he says. "I used to live here!" He can't contain himself. He's beaming, he's growing misty, he loves me for living here. He's maybe seventy, big but not terribly fat, ironed shirt, polyester pants, clean socks and Birkenstock sandals, hairy arms, bald head, hairy neck, hairy chest, all hair white, skin of his face robustly pink and healthy, soulful eyes, brown:

"Hi!" I say. I'm catching his emotion, his exclamation points.

"Oh Lord!" he says.

Now the woman gets out of the car. She's younger than he, built large, lots of dark hair, pretty. Suddenly, Tom Q. Moonrobin is in tears. The woman comforts him and pats his back and nods her head. She's warm and sweet and big as he is. "I'm Tom's wife," she says.

"She's a minister," Tom blubbers.

"I'm pastor of the Stonecoast Methodist," she says without undue pride.

"Oh Lord!" Tom says again.

His wife pats him. "He hasn't been back," she tells me. "This is his first time back."

"We better go," Tom blubbers. "We're bothering you."

"Oh, no, no, no." I say. "Look around."

"You've fixed it up," Tom says, still blubbering.

"Not only I," I tell him, wanting to be like his wife—no undue pride.

He asks my name. I give it. He tells me he's heard of Pete Johnson, knew the California Couple to whom he'd sold in such a hurry had sold out quickly thence, but this! A new owner! He composes himself, smiles broadly, embarrassed. "You love this place!" he says.

"I do," I say, and it's true: I love it with all my heart.

"Oh, Lord! My wife passed away here!" he says abruptly, and breaks down into sobs once more.

"This is very important to him," his new wife says, somewhat chagrined. She pats him. "You're very kind," she says.

"I'm just here," I say.

"We'll go," she says.

"No, let's look around," I say.

"Oh, Lord!" Tom wails, a plaint for all humankind, for all history. But he's stopped crying.

"I'll wait in the car," his wife says, the minister. "This is for you, darling."

So Tom and I walk the grounds. It's terrific; he knows all the answers. He slowly contains his emotion: "Those trees? I planted them! They were only just this high!" Now the row of balsam firs looms forty feet in the air, too close together, grown solid into the windbreak he'd pictured. "That was the sugar house," he says pointing at the Johnson girls' playhouse. "I built it of wood from the stable, which we tore down—'twas right here!"

A stable explained all the horseshoes.

"Our pig was here!" Thomas C. Moonrobin says. He's grown plump. He reminds me of my dad. He's sweet like my dad where I'd pictured from the evidence a tough guy. He's so happy to be here. He's exorcising his horrible grief. He's newly wed, he tells me. She's a minister, he tells me again. "I've never got over it!" he says. "How I loved this place!" He says, "I never ever thought I'd leave it ever!" He points to the larch tree, a tamarack, in the side yard, and says, using the local name, "That's my rackmatack! Kelly and me, we . . . ," and he's a fountain of tears. "Oh, I'm sorry," he moans.

"It's wonderful to have you," I tell him.

He explains how the VW body got into the hollow with the older cars. He points out every shrub he planted. He remembers where things are buried, where the old well was, the outhouse. It was he who brought plumbing to this olden place. Four kids he and Mary raised! "Oh Lord!" And he's in tears again. Such a lovely man, so full of feeling. I want to pat him as his wife has done, but can't quite do it. His shirt is nice, cotton, blue stripes. He's not what I pictured from the evidence at all.

"I have some tools of yours," I say.

"No!" he says. "No, no, no! They are yours, now. I left everything! I just packed and left, one carload of stuff and whatever the boys got into their cars and we left!"

Oh Lord, is right. We stand in the side yard and he just gazes around. Thirty-two years he lived here and raised four kids. We walk around front of the house. The minister, his new wife, is reading a heavy magazine in the front seat of their minivan. She's in her forties, is my guess, plump and serious and pretty, a nice wife for him. At the front door he just stares. You can see in the window there, can see right through the stairwell-foyer and through the parlor and all the way back and through the bathroom windows into the yard.

"You've done some things," he says.

I don't have to say a word.

"Things I wanted to do. I'm so happy about that."

"Come on in," I say.

"Oh Lord!" he says. And he breaks down into barking, wailing cries, his hands on his knees. Now I do pat his back. Pat pat pat. I pat his back and he's big as my father, who has started crying lately too.

"Oh Lord!" he wails.

His wife hears him and gets placidly out of the car and comes over placidly and takes over patting his back. "He never once cried in the sixteen years since," she says.

He slowly subsides as we stand there the three of us under our big healthy elm tree, slowly stands straight. "Oh Lord," he says. "I wasn't expecting this," he says.

"This man wasn't either," says his wife to me kindly.

"I'm fine," I say, but I'm moved, too, I mean, tears in my eyes threatening to fall.

My lachrymose predecessor hugs me, and I hug him.

"Oh Lord!" he says, one more time, letting me go.

"You don't want to go in?" says the new wife.

"Simply couldn't," he says, sobbing.

"Come back sometime," I say.

"No," he says. "We won't."

"Come to Stonecoast Village," says his wife.

They get in their car and drive off, and I go back to the Johnson girls' oak tree, resume my mortal task.

Shitdiggers, Mudflats, and the Worm Men of Maine

"Hard work," says Dicky Butts, and we haven't even started yet.

"Get wet today," says Truman Lock. He pulls his graying beard, squints out over the bay. The blast of an offshore wind (strong enough to blow the boat and its no-lights trailer halfway into the oncoming lane as we made the drive over) is piling whitecaps, spraying their tops, bowing the trees around us, knocking my hat off my head, giving even the wormers pause.

Dicky says, "No fun today."

Walter—Truman's father—lets a long minute go by, says, "We do get some weather, Downeast." He seems to know he's offering a cliche, works the rich inflections of his Maine twang extra hard: there's an observer here, myself, and no one (including me) knows exactly what the observer wants.

The night's rain has stopped and the cold front that caused it is finishing its push. The dirt parking area at the shore access on Ripley Neck is nearly empty—most of the wormers have decided to let this tide go—too much like March (here toward the last days of June)—too wild, too easy to stay in bed. "Not a climber in the lot," Truey says, one of a constant stream of plain observations. It'll take me fifty conversations with twenty wormdiggers before I figure out the obvious: a climber is a clammer. He means most of the usual guys aren't here today—clammers, crabbers, inside lobstermen, wormers—not even anybody picking weed. Just two cars in the lot—mature Subarus, both of them—no boat trailers.

We watch the tide. It will be a big one, Truey guesses, with the offshore wind blowing the bay empty. He's sitting at the wheel of his Chevy truck, Dicky at his side. Walter and I stand in the parking lot at their two windows. We all watch the bay. Low water is charted at 7:30 this morning. It's six now. We watch, and watch more. That's what we do, watch. No talking. Down on the mudflats a quarter-mile away a couple of men are bent low, visibly chopping at the mud with their worm hoes. "Bloods," Truey says.

"Those boys are blood wormers," Dicky says, deciding to pull me in a little, help me out here, whatever I'm up to. He's a stocky, good-looking man with a naked lady tattooed on one arm, a faded bird in a flower on the other. At thirty-three, he's the youngest of the team. He has a wide face and ought to look jolly, but he doesn't. Jolly you need to smile. He's taciturn and tough, burned and blown, his skin newly cooked over a deep spring tan, the creases of his neck white. He's got mud smears on the bill of his no-team baseball cap. You think maybe he's a little mean until he speaks and, yes, finally smiles, but it's a warm smile, not jolly at all in the wide face, a good father's smile, and you see how kindly he is, how helpful. This he wants to avoid showing. He pronounces the word wormers—names his profession—with softened r's and extra vowels, points out the bent men, says, "Ten cents a worm." Back to taciturn.

Ten chops, ten deep turns of the mud, a pause to pull a worm, ten more chops, drop a worm in the bucket. Ten chops bent over the heavy muck and those guys out there get a dime, a dime a worm, 100 weary chops to a dollar, 1000 chops for ten bucks, 10,000 chops to make the tide pay.

"Those fellows are Garneys," Walter says. He knows every wormer in Washington County by sight, and probably most in the state. He's been at this forever. He wants me to know that a Garney is any digger from Beal's Island, which is just over the bridge from Jonesport, a few miles east. He wants me to know that the Beal's Island boys are known for working in bad weather, and for working low tide all the way up to the beach, staying in the mud longer than maybe is good for the worm population. But then, every wormer wants you to know that every other wormer is a fuckhead. I'm thinking of a certain group of Midcoast boys who told me how dumb and lazy the Downeast boys are, including these very boys right here.

"Shitdiggers," Dicky spits. It sounds like genuine animosity, but if I said it I'd probably get a blood rake through the brain.

Truey pulls the muddy brim of his cap, patiently fills me in: "Sandworms, see, are but six cents, but it's faster getting. Those guys out there was here an hour before us. They'll be here an hour longer for their money, and rip the mud right to the weed line."

"It does takes a toll on your back," Walter says dreamily, apropos of nothing in particular.

Oh, fuck. I'm here on a magazine assignment: get to know these guys, these peculiar wormers, these strugglers at the extreme end of our great economy, write a poignant piece about their miserable lives. But they don't seem miserable. Not as miserable as I am, for example, doing a job I'm really anxious about, inside a nascent career I'm really anxious about, a shaky career that has me saying yes to assignments like this, so many cents a word, really not the kind of thing I'm good at. For one thing, I'm feeling horribly guilty, stealing these guys' lives from them, worried sick what they'll think of their portraits when the magazine hits the racks in town. No one likes his own picture.

But here we are, all of us doing our work in this beautiful, dramatic place. Which is their place, one they know intimately, a place they know themselves to belong. They are their own economy, efficient, dependable, always bears, always bulls. Get to know them? They aren't going to let that happen unless I'm willing to work a couple of years alongside them, and probably not then. I've found Truey after an unbelievably long series of phone conversations with mistrustful Yankees, Truey the one wormer in all of Downeast Maine who said, sure, sure, come along and worm.

"Bloodworms," Truey sighs, not with malice, exactly, but with the supercilious pride of a specialist: these fellows dig sandworms, and even if maybe they are less hardy, less appealing to fish, less marketable and so less valuable, they're easier to come by. He keeps looking me up and down. I smile too much, smile now.

This is not my first day worming. I had a day up Midcoast with a bunch of mean-spirited mo-fo's. Shitdiggers, for sure. The Midcoast boys abused me, rightfully so: what comes to them for talking to me? But more about them soon. Right now I'm Downeast, anxious but hopeful. Months have passed since my Midcoast frolic without much progress on my story. My big break is slipping away. Truey and Dicky and Walter are my last chance. And a new strategy is in place: I haven't told them specifically about *Harper's*, only that I'm a professor at the University of Maine at Farmington, doing a kind of study of guys working, and that I'll write about them. All true. They maybe expected a pipe, a tweed jacket, elbow patches, a vaguely British accent. Instead they got me: UMF sweatshirt, long hair, guy basically their age, a *classic* summer dink and a flatlander to boot.

Truey looks me over thoroughly, maybe trying to think what will interest me. He nods in the direction of one of the Subarus in the empty parking lot: "That's Porky Bob. He's a climber, most generally, but they just ain't any steamers, not anymore. He'll be digging bloods, today."

I'm rumpled and desperately bleary, slept poorly maybe three hours in the Blueberry Motel, the only motel open this time of year anywhere near, lone customer, windy night.

"They would used to get ten bushels," Walter says, "a whole pickup load on a tide. Now you're lucky with a plateful for supper." He looks pained and weary. "It's the pollution. It's the runoff from the blueberry highlands."

This does interest me. I'm nodding my head earnestly.

"Some say sewerage," Truey says.

"No," Walter says. "That's the lie. The clam, he likes the sewage. What he don't like is the sewage treatment."

"Many a wormer was once a climber," Truey says.

The three men leave me out now, rapid shoptalk. I hear it the way I hear Spanish: pick out words here and there, get the drift. They're speculating about the worm population at Pigeon Hill, which I know to be a beach up toward Hancock. They're bad-mouthing some climber. They're thinking the weather will clear. They're speculating about the take today. They're talking about urchins, near as I can tell, something spirited about sea urchins and the frukking Japanese. Walter would rather eat pussy than that stuff. But Jack Morrison made $2800 in a day diving for 'em. And Truey's a certified diver. The rest sounds like daydreaming: all they need is scuba, an urchin boat (forty feet would do 'er), hot tanks for divers (the deep water in the Gulf of Maine is brutally cold in every season), some of that stuff is all, and you make $2800 a day.

Without a word of transition, without a word at all, Truey is pulling his truck around in the ominously empty parking lot, listening all the while to some story Dicky is telling, then backing the Cox trailer smoothly and straight as a new ashen oar down the steep ramp to the bay. Walter plods down behind, thinking of something else, chewing a thumbnail. I march down after him, flopping in my new worming boots (the Downeast salesman pronounced this *women* boots), anxious to be of use. But these aren't vacationers nervous at the winch of their thousand-buck trailer, this is Truey and Dicky knocking a scarred plank of junkyard lumber out from under the motor (a muddy Mercury 200, no messing around, a good old machine much reworked by Truey, who's a local stock-car racer, and Dicky, who's his mechanic): knock the plank, unhook the cable, let the boat hit the water, no splash. Now three of us are at the gunwales (I imitate every gesture they make, trying to be useful), waiting for Truey to park his mostly orange truck and return.

Dicky grins at me. "Gonna get wet," he says. He sees my thin sweatshirt and that I don't have a raincoat and yells up to Truey to bring what they got. He's so solicitous I stop worrying about the high wind. I stop thinking about the low-down, blood-worming, shit-digging Midcoast boys who laughed and left me stuck in the mud, laughed derisively and chopped across the mud away from me, giggling like middle-aged and tattooed twelve-year-olds, dunking worms in their buckets, dunking worms. I stop thinking about my deadline, two weeks past, stop worrying that my worming story is going to get killed. (In the end, okay, it did get killed, but me, I've got the experience of worming under my belt, my fat kill fee, and my own blood-worm rake, which will hang forevermore in the shed at my inland house.)

"This weather'll clear by noon," Walter says, watching the sky. He's built small and strong, is always preoccupied, always has a subject in mind and an informed, unexpected opinion ("If them senators up in Washington was all women, we'd have our troubles solved."). He's not only a wormdigger but his wife's partner as a minor worm dealer. His own dad (recently dead of diabetes, from which Walter also suffers) was a wormer, too, one of the originals up in Wiscasset with worming legends Bill and Artie Wanser and Frank Hammond—the first guys in the business back when the war was over and life was sweet and anybody could be Ernest Hemingway—go sportfishing in the ocean—anybody anywhere in the world: customers.

Truey returns with an armless orange sweatshirt for me and a torn yellow slicker. "All we have extra," he says, with real concern. He's got muscles and the same gruff demeanor as Dicky, and like Dicky he's warm and helpful and kind, all that just hiding behind a stern self-possession that you might read as distrust. But he's got a certain coldness to him, the bluff chill of the bad father. His cap says Mrs. Giant Jim's Street Stock on it. Mrs. Giant Jim's Pizza, up on Route 1, is one of his racing sponsors. In Mrs. Giant Jim's they've got pictures of Truey in his lemon-yellow number five, holding the checkered flag after big wins at Bangor Speedway, never a smile for the camera.

I put the partial sweatshirt and ripped slicker on gratefully and the three wormers look at me a long time the way they've been looking at the tide: not much they can do about either, not much at all. We get in the boat, a twenty-one-foot aluminum camo-painted Quachita flat-bottom workboat full of worming stuff: four blood hoes, four sandworm hoes, three wormboxes, four buckets, several twisted blue gloves, one faded green one, three life preservers, first aid kit.

We're off. Truey's the helmsman, Dicky beside him, both of them standing. Walter and I are on the middle seat facing forward, taking the spray.

I examine my women boots. Last time out, with the japing Midcoast boys, I wore my fly-fishing hip boots, which have thick felt soles for traction on mossy river rocks. The deep tidal mud up by Bar Harbor sucked them off my feet over and over again till they were gone. So now I've got better boots, the real thing, according to Walter (who has explained that they're "Number one in Maine"): tight-ankle LaCrosse hip waders. I've gotten them two sizes small to be sure of their snugness. I wonder if I should have tied strips of inner tube around the arches, as Walter also suggested, but I don't want to look like a total fucking dork. I start to tie and button the interior calf straps (a collar of eyes inside the boot below the knee that you tighten like shoelaces before you pull the thighs up), aware that Walter is too preoccupied to notice what I'm up to.

Dicky is staring. He says, "I myself personally prefer not to use the calf straps."

I say I don't want to get stuck in the mud, tell him the Midcoast story.

He and Truey grin at the picture of me floundering as the Midcoast boys leave me behind, especially the part where my ass is in the mud and I have to let go of my notebook and pen, losing them, then losing the boots. Har har har, then my new friends fall back into their default faces—pretty grim—let me finish tying the calves of my boots.

Dicky says, "If we go in you need to get them boots off pretty fast . . ."

"Ah," Truey says, "We ain't going in."

Walter isn't listening, is looking to where we are going. He points, says, "Some mud showing over there."

Truey says, "Benson Williams."

Dicky says, "Little Fred."

Truey says, "That fellow from Jackman."

These are people who have indeed "gone in." The tone isn't quite elegiac, but before I can ask for elaboration, Walter's telling Truey to slow down. There's a flotilla of lobster buoys, for one thing (which, to be sure, Truey has been missing expertly); for another, these waves will be big trouble if he gets the boat up planing. Truey nods with an irritated patience and you can see Walter has been giving him advice like this for a lifetime. Truey's forty, now. His dad is fifty-seven. Truey's name is actually Walter, too—Walter Lock III—but he was born on Harry Truman's birthday.

We are in the estuarine bay of the Harrington River, heading for Foster Island below Ray Point. I've gotten these names off of maps, for in the manner of most people deeply familiar with their surroundings, Walter and Truey and Dicky can't quite remember the names of the islands and spits and necks around us, only that good worming can be found on the flats that will appear here shortly. They venture several guesses, but can't agree on the names. Finally Walter says if you were to boat around the island you'd end up at Milbridge, the next town up the coast (up being toward Portland, which is a hundred miles south and west).

We're crashing over waves now. Truey and Dicky crouch a little, but stay on their feet in the stern. The old gas tank, less than a quarter full, bounces around back there. Walter kneels on the middle seat beside me. We all look resolutely forward. The spray is ice cold. I think of hackneyed Maine-coast paintings, proceed to compose one: five stripes of color—the gray plane of clouds, the green of the pines in the shore forest, the naked gray rocks, the brown rockweed exposed by the tide, water the gray of the sky but alive with whitecaps. We're the sole boat today; the scene is dramatic, timeless, lacks color, a Wyeth, which generation of Wyeth I'm not sure.

Our beeline has brought us across Harrington Bay to several hundred yards off Foster Island. Truey lifts the motor and we skim onto the mud. Again we sit and watch. You can see disturbed places in the exposed muck. "That is yesterday," Dicky says. "That is us." The wind is so strong I have to pull my San Francisco Giants cap down to my eyebrows, cock my head. I don't know why San Francisco—it's just a hat, but Dicky looks at the logo all day rather than in my eyes, asks me on the way home if it's a Chinese character on there.

"See them two?" Truey says. He's pointing out men I hadn't noticed, crouched men chopping at the mud much closer to shore. I don't at first see their boat, and ask how they got there.

"Canoe," Dicky says.

"Wouldn't be in a canoe today," Walter says. He hops out of the boat, overboard into the mud. From the bow he collects his sandworm hoe (what climbers might call a rake)—five claw-curved steel tines nineteen inches long, these welded onto a bar that is welded in turn onto a post that impales a wooden handle about nine inches long. The angle between handle and hoe is sharp; at work, one's knuckles are just behind the tines. Walter has shaped his handle to fit his stiffened fingers; the carving is artful: skin-smooth, oiled, comfortable. Next he hefts his wormbox, a homemade fiberglass case like a carpenter's box mixed with a budget cooler, fitted at top with the wooden handle from a broom. Attached to one end is a big old coffee can—a vessel for bloodworms, which sandwormers view as incidental, but which bring ten cents each—it's not like you're going to throw them away. He slides the box along the mud, leans forward, moves fast enough to keep from sinking beyond the point of suction. I study his style. He's a strong old guy, moves with grace through the mud.

"Watch him," Truey says, "he'll dig all around the mussel beds," this with a mix of affectionate pride and irritation at his dad's predictability. And sure enough, Walter is into the edges of the mussel bed, which is slowly coming exposed with the tide. He operates knee-deep in the muck, digging and stepping, moving his wormbox along beside him. Each big flip of mud seems to produce a worm. He holds them up one by one for me to see.

"Rattlesnake," Truey says, making fun, since Walter claims the mussel-bed worms are bigger.

"Tinker," Dicky says.

"Shitdigger," Truey taunts, and we all briefly laugh. I miss the switch back to grim, find myself laughing alone.

Walter slogs speedily off across the mud to the next mussel bed. Dicky and Truey and I wait. We wait a little more. Truey points out the bloodwormers again. "Man in the red is the fastest wormer Downeast," he says. "You watch him go." It's true, the man is chopping three strokes a second, stepping along the mud, a hundred yards ahead of his partner, hundreds of yards from his canoe.

"That fellow lost his son this spring," Dicky says. "Day pretty well like this."

We watch the man work. He does not straighten periodically as his partner does; he does not rest.

"Six hundred pounds of wrinkles," Truey says. "Boy and his partner. Was he twenty-one yet? Six hundred pounds of wrinkles in the bottom of their canoe. *Six hundred* pounds."

"Got turned by the wind," Dicky says. His own son is twelve, and for now Dicky gives him half the summer off. "The boy was not a swimmer. Though his partner made it all right."

"They should have went to college," Truey says. He's eyeing me closely, this professor, right here in his worm boat. Dicky, too, more subtly.

This is a test. I don't give a twitch, not a smile. I say, "That's a sad story."

We watch the bloodwormer, watch him digging like hell, plopping worms in his bucket, chopping the mud.

Dicky says, "College is not for everybody."

"True," I say.

I'm off the hook.

The wind has picked up. It's singing in my ears, watering my eyes. I'm thinking of the boy sinking in his boots. I ask what wrinkles are, exactly. Truey sighs, twirls his finger to draw the creature in the air, makes me to understand that wrinkles are those little spiral-shelled snails, what I have always called periwinkles. He says, "The Japanese eat 'em. I wouldn't go near 'em." You can't quite tell if he means the snails or the Japanese. His sons are babies, still, two and four, products of his third marriage.

"Nor is worming," Dicky says. Nor is it for everybody, he means.

We watch the sky, watch the tide, sit in the boat in the wind. No warning and the guys are overboard, grabbing their wormboxes and hoes. Truey asks if I'm blooding or sanding. I say sanding—of course—and they give me a hoe and a bucket. I pull my women boots up to my thighs, tie the ties into my belt loops, and step overboard. I sink. I step. I've got the bucket and the hoe. I sink, step, sink, step, suckingly follow the men. Step, sink, looking for the little round holes that signal sandworm mud. When Dicky crouches to the task I watch him. Strike the tines full depth into the mud (nineteen inches!), two hands to turn the heavy gray stuff, a quick grab to pick out the worms, one or two or three to every dig in this spot. Good mud. Three or four digs, then step.

"The trick is to keep moving," Truey says. The two of them are off, leaving four-foot wide swaths of turned mud behind them, digging, digging, plucking worms, sliding the worm-boxes—lean forward steeply and step—dig right, dig left, dig middle, pluck worms, step.

I use two hands, grunt and turn the mud. My back already hurts. Two worms. I tug on one where it's escaping back into its hole in the mud and it breaks, pull on the other more carefully and it comes free—a foot long, orangey brown, cilia down its length, appearance of a flattened and softened centipede, perhaps a half-inch in diameter, diameter turning to width as the worm flattens trying to locomote out of my hand. Dicky has given me his gloves, so I'm not worried about the stingers hidden in the retracted head. I put the worm in my bucket. *One.* Next chop and I note the tunnels the worms leave— slightly discolored tubes in the mud. The worms can move very quickly into the un-dug, disappear. You chop and grab. You don't wait around. *Two.* You step. *Three.* I'm doing fine, not stuck, proud of my new boots. Chop, two hands. The stuff is heavy. I'm glad I'm strong, wish I were stronger, remember how I've bragged to Juliet that I'm in great shape. *Four, five, six.*

"Those little digs'll hurt your back," Truey advises, kindly. He's ten feet ahead of me already.

Dicky has walked to a new spot, far to my right. "Try to make it all one scoop." He shows me—swoop, scoop—plops worms into his bucket.

I make a big dig, do it right, turn a great chunk of mud, watch the hole grow wet, look in there for movement. I pull out an odd, long, flat worm that just keeps coming—three feet long, at a guess.

"Tapeworm," Truey says. He very nearly smiles, because tapeworms are ridiculous, useless.

I dig again, showing Truey every worm I turn, trying to get the sense of an acceptable size. The worms expand in length then quickly retract, so you can't really put it in inches. You just have to know. Truey okays a couple, shrugs at a third. The shrug is as negative as he'll get with me. Next worm is a blood. Truey turns back to his work: the tide is only low enough for two-and-a-half or three hours of digging this far out on the flat—you can't socialize. I examine the bloodworm, which is wholly different from a sandworm. No cilia, for one thing, and it's all pink translucence, smaller than a sand, more substantial than an earthworm, something deeply red beneath the surface of its skin. This one is smallish, not quite six inches, with a thickening at the head end, a bit of flattening at the tail. I roll it in my fingers. Abruptly, the head shoots out, a moist pink cylinder an inch long, ugly and sudden, un-benign, bulging and unfolding till the stingers show, four grasping needles in the circle of the nasty mouth. Walter has told me that if they get you in the webs between your fingers your whole hand'll blow right up. I haven't been worried till now—how bad could a worm bite be? Bad, is the answer. I let the worm grasp at the air a moment, then throw it in with the sandworms in my bucket—a mistake, as I will discover: the bloods bite the sandworms in half, making them worthless.

Step and dig, dig and step; my legs are growing exhausted, forty feet from the boat. The digging style Truey showed me seems to be saving my back, though. Dig and step. I've lost count of my take, but it looks like a lot in there—a crawling, wriggling, spiraling mass, sunken in the quart of seawater I've added to the mix. There's quite a bit of mud in there too. Incredibly, I don't turn up a single clam. Incredibly, I forget about my assignment. My notebook never comes out of my pocket. I'm worming.

The wind is getting stronger yet, and colder, takes my San Francisco Giants cap. I lunge for it, fall in the mud, get the hat, put it dripping on my head, manage to stand by leaning hard on bucket with one hand, rake with the other. I wish for the sandy flats Walter has told me he used to work with his dad, up past Portland by George Bush's place, all along and up to Kennebunkport. You can't get near there now.

Step and dig. Dig and step. It's getting harder and harder to lift my feet. I keep needing to stand straight, but it's standing that gets you stuck. Suddenly, a mudhole boils in front of me. Before I can react, an eel pops out, leaps from his hole and into my face, struggles away, gets a few feet and pauses, gills gaping. I give a little scream of surprise.

"Oh yes," Truey calls. He's farther away from me yet.

"Mud eel," Dicky shouts in the wind.

The seagulls descend, laughing. The eel slithers back in my direction.

"He's a meal," Truey shouts. He means the eel, for the seagulls.

I stop and watch the spectacle, seagulls, eel, the wind, the waves away off where the mud stops, the plane of dramatic clouds, the salty and sulfuric smell of the mud, the men working methodically away from me. I'm this close to having some sort of college-professor epiphany when I realize I've gazed too long. I'm stuck.

I look back at the boat—it's far. I look at Dicky and Truman and know I've got to get out on my own. I hear in my head the Midcoast boys' derisive laughter. I struggle. My mud muscles—some rare strands in the sides and tops of my thighs—are exhausted, can't do it. I pull with my hands on the lip of my right boot, get it to move a little. I pull on my left, but my foot leaves the boot and won't go back in. I remember Truey's story about Crawford Peacham's moronic son—how the dumb kid got stuck and they had to cut his boots off 'im. How the kid was covered with mud, mud in his nostrils, mud in his mouth, mud halfway up the frukkin' wazoo. I wriggle and pull and both socks are off inside the boots and both boots are stuck and I'm not connected to them except at the calves, where I'm firmly laced. I fall over, go up to my elbows in the mud, then very slowly up to my biceps. Both arms, both legs. Soon it'll be my face. Deadline two weeks gone. I'm sinking.

"He's stuck," Truey calls.

Dicky looks back, and just when you think the laughter should erupt the two of them are dropping their hoes and coming at me, almost racing. Truey gets there first and without a word pulls my arms out, stands me up, then puts his strong hands under my knees and yanks me free a leg at a time, oblivious of the gazes the bloodwormers downflat turn our way.

Dicky makes a forward-leaning race to the boat, pushes it over the mud in a mighty effort, brings it right up behind me so I can sit on the port gunwale. The two of them inspect me a moment, then go back to work without a tease of any kind. I sit in the boat a long time, getting my socks back on, getting my boots readjusted, resting my thighs and my back, getting the mud off my face. The whole time I keep my eye on a certain small hummock of mussels, watch it closely the way as a stock boy I used to watch the clock at the A&P, watch relieved as the hummock sinks in the returning tide.

"Did he quit?" Truey shouts over the wind.

"I think he quit," Dicky calls back. There's no doubt I better go back to work. I climb out of the boat, dig my way close around it in a big rectangle, afraid to move far from the safety of its gunwales. I chop and step and pluck and pull. It's like digging nickels out of the fetid mud, pennies. It's like freelance writing. Forget it.

⟋

Near Ellsworth, back in April, back when the deadline for my article was still months off, back before I'd found Truey and Walter and Dicky by telephone, back when I didn't know how many television stations and local papers and even *Yankee Magazine* had done stories on worming using the same Midcoast boys repeatedly, back when my ridiculous plan was to go out on the flats alone, hoping to meet fellow wormers, back then I drove down to a town near Ellsworth that I shall, with no great prejudice, call Wormville, drove all morning to pop into the Town Hall in this little coastal town—Town Hall being a well-kept colonial-era house—popped in, all fake confidence, all grins and swagger, to ask about a worming license.

"Who're you digging for?" the Wormville Town Clerk said, all smiles herself.

I faltered a little at the unexpected question, said, "Just digging?"

Now the Town Clerk was all frowns. She listened to my convoluted explanation of mission skeptically (UMF professor, writing about working men in Maine, meet the real guys out on the flats), but in the end she had to hand me a license application—all Maine residents are eligible—one form for all of the many Maine-coast commercial fisheries.

Later, over a lobster lunch at Ruth and Wimpy's incredible Lobster Shack, I would check off the box for marine worm digging, add my birthdate, height and weight. Later still I'd cheerfully write a check for $43.00, cheerful because *Harper's* would pay (and pay for my worm rake, and various horrid motels, and maybe a dozen lobsters at Ruth and Wimpy's, at least that, even if the story got killed), cheerfully mail the whole thing off to the department of Marine Resources in Augusta, which (as I would note with my newly acquired wormdigger's churlishness) isn't even on the coast. But right now, having provided me with all I needed to get started, the good Town Clerk of Wormville walked me to the Town Hall door and pointed across the street to one of the few other commercial buildings in town, a modern, one-story affair with a pair of handsomely carved-and-painted wood signs: the first, Gulf of Maine Bait Company; the second, Gulf of Maine Wreath Company. She said, "Before you go drowning yourself on the flats you'll want to talk to Nelson Forrest," and was rid of me.

I walked over and was intercepted in the parking lot by Nelson Forrest himself, energetically on his way somewhere else. I rather nervously explained what I was after, using the whole professor bit, interested in the work, etc., still saying nothing about *Harper's*, or any national article. But here, finally, after two weeks of fruitless phone calls looking for sources, looking for reporterly access to the world of worming, I had someone live to talk to. Mr. Forrest seemed preoccupied, even a little annoyed, but once he got me in his office—thin paneling, tidy old desk, real oil paintings (appealingly amateur), smell of the sea, a phone, a fax—he leaned back in his chair, lit a cigarette, became voluble, answering questions I hadn't asked: "State law says the worms must be dug by hand." He's well tanned and much creased, his eyes blue as the sky over Cadillac Mountain on Mt. Desert Island (pronounced *dessert* as in deserter), which is due south, just across Frenchman Bay. To folks in Wiscasset,

Wormville is Downeast. To folks Downeast, Wormville is Mid-coast. Wiscasset might as well be Massachusetts.

Mr. Forrest stares intently at me, talks rapidly, explains the business, answering his own questions: "We pay ten cents a worm for bloods. Six cents for sands. Up in Wiscasset they're paying twelve cents, but they have less shipping cost." The diggers, whom Forrest carefully calls independent contractors, bring the worms to one of ten or fifteen dealers—places like Gulf of Maine Bait—for counting, starting about an hour after low water ("They'll stagger in for hours after that," he says, then corrects himself: "Well not stagger, exactly"). On vinyl-covered tables the men (and a few women) count bloods rapidly into wooden trays of 250, then fill out a card:

250 BLOOD WORMS
dug and counted by:

_____

Forrest also deals sandworms, but far fewer: "I hate sand-worms; they're so frigging fragile. They'll die if you look at 'em." He transfers the worms to newspaper-and-seaweed-lined cardboard flats, where they rest in the walk-in cooler to wait for the worm van, a service provided by several independent shippers (Great Northern Seafood, for one example: "Worm Transit, Maine to Maryland"). Nelson's worms—3,000 to 15,000 a day—are driven to Logan airport, and from there flown to points south (Maryland, Virginia, North Carolina), west (California, especially Sacramento) and east (Mediterranean France, Spain, and Italy). "It's a unique business. You tell people you sell worms . . . they look at you." The wholesale buyers are either distributors who service bait shops or the captains of fishing charters. The final price out there in the world—some guy fishing for sea bass or spot or weakfish or flounder—is in the range of three to four dollars a dozen. Mr. Forrest nods proudly: "They do catch fish. See, they're two-thirds blood. Maybe it's the scent, we don't know." His competition, in his estimation, isn't other worm dealers, really, but twenty-four other ocean baits including eels, sea clams, herring, and squid. Of these, squid is probably the most effective, and, unlike worms, can be frozen for shipment, then frozen again by the fisherman after partial use. "Worms aren't the distributors' favorite," Mr. Forrest says, "they die, they're expensive . . . but they need 'em."

Terrible years, good years, the business seems to go on, though not like the old days. Nelson Forrest, who has never dug worms himself, wriggled into worming back in 1972—boom times. He shakes his head about the terrible years of the late eighties—tiny worms, and not many—won't venture a theory as to where the big ones went, though (like every cycle in business and nature), the sea-worm cycle does have its theorists. Pollution plays a role in many of these visions, overharvesting in others. Global warming gets a nod, and one strident wormer I talked to up near Wiscasset invoked Chernobyl (but oddly not the defunct Yankee nuclear facility, which is right in Wiscasset's backyard). Some don't see doom, particularly, just the well-known fact that sea worms are unpredictable. Some years there are plenty of big ones, the kind the fishermen like, some years there just ain't. Nelson Forrest would like to see some conservation—maybe close the mud in winter, maybe think more about size limits. "It's a constant battle to keep the guys out of the little ones . . . and we don't buy on Sundays." He pauses, considers. "Though that's no conservation measure; the guys just refrigerate Sunday worms, bring 'em in Monday." Then he shakes his head, lights the fifth cigarette of our conversation. "When I started, I worried I'd be out of worms in ten years." He looks at me carefully, to see that I'm not missing the point, shakes his head again: "But we're running out of fish first. The fish are *gone*. Pollution, commercial overfishing, this frigging *economy*—they do destroy sportfishing." And where sportfishing goes, the wormers will go.

That afternoon there's a 2:30 tide, and Mr. Forrest sets me up with one of his crews, the group I have been calling the Midcoast boys, these fellows who, I'll later learn, are practically worming *poster* boys they've been on TV so much. They love nothing more than razzing a guy with a tie and a microphone. The wormers know something most reporters won't admit: they're getting used. But torturing a reporter for a tide can make up for it, make time fly.

One of the crew, my guide, gets me to follow him in my own vehicle—sixty miles an hour on back roads to one Thompson Island. I watch his head turn at every sight of the water; he's checking the size of the tide, driving off the road. We park on the main drag into Bar Harbor in front of an enormous fence that hides a gargantuan house.

After I've donned my fly-fishing boots in the face of my guide's skeptical impatience (but no warnings), he trots me past two no-trespassing signs and through the summer-dink lawn, around a summer-dink gate and past two more summer-dink property signs, then along an old lane through a quiet wood, shore pines and pin oaks, lots of poison ivy. Past the fifth and sixth no-trespassing signs we break into a little meadow that is on a point thrust into the Mount Desert Narrows. Trap Rock is in sight, and Thomas Island. Seals play out there. There's a strong onshore breeze, the sound of waves crashing, white sprays of foam thrown up on rocks out there. It's gorgeous.

In the cover of some scruffy pines and under yet another no-trespassing sign, three grim guys await. My guide offers no introductions. I pull out my little notebook filled with little questions to ask, but every one of them looks and sounds like it was written at four in the morning in the worst motel in Ellsworth. We all of us stand amongst boulders and birch trees and watch the tide, which for me means picking out a particular rock and keeping track of how wet it is.

I smile my rube's smile. "So what are your all's names?"

Nothing.

"You. Hi. Where do you live?"

Nada.

"How much can a good wormer expect to make on the average tide?"

Silence.

"Ever get into fights over territory?"

Here we go. They all look at me. My guide says, "Old days you'd have a hell of a brawl. Now we see guys from Wiscasset or someplace, we might holler some."

"Tell 'em to *go the fuck* home," the next guy says, real fury.

My guide says, "Used to be you'd shoot holes in a guy's boat."

Another gently says, "Tires do get slashed. But some years the worms are one place and not another and fellows travel."

"Where're *you* from?" the go-the-fuck-home guy says. Everyone looks at me closely.

Me, I don't say a thing, just look out at the tide.

"He's from the college," my guide says. "Farmington, up there."

"I thought only queers lived up that way!"

I'm supposed to defend Farmington, I guess. But I don't. What am I going to say? *Well, yes, we have some gay citizens, of course, about ten percent, I believe, something along those lines, same as Wormville, same as anywhere. Nice folks, our queers. Get used to it!*

We stand on the rocks. We watch the tide. The breeze itself feels tense, carries drops of rain. Where's the story? I don't say a word. The men around me stiffen.

Shoptalk saves the day. My guide says, "She gonna go out?"

The gentle man says, "Somewhat, I think." That onshore wind will keep the tide small.

The angry fellow says, "Probably under eight feet."

My guide: "Shit tide."

The angry fellow: "I'll give you ten bucks you bail out the bay."

They all snigger and have a look at me to see if I believe that's possible. I notice for the first time that the silent man is a young teen. He looks as if he feels sorry for me. I love him for that, gangly kid. He stands half behind the protection of his dad's back (his dad is the gentle one), holding a bloodworm hoe (six tines nine inches long, short wooden handle), dangles it at the end of one limp arm, an empty joint-compound bucket dangled at the end of the other, the tools of the trade looking like mittens someone has pinned to his jacket.

"You like worming?" I ask him inanely.

"I'm just doing it so my dad don't get pissed off when I ask for *money*."

His dad doesn't laugh, stares the boy down.

Around a corner on the rocky mud toward the mainland a lone figure comes a-slogging, a stately, slow march through the muck, his bucket in one hand, hoe in the other. On shore he'd look weary; on firm land he'd look gimpy and stiff; on dry land he'd be another old salt spitting stories; but on the flats there's a grandeur about him. He pauses and looks at the mud, continues on, pauses and looks at the mud, stoops, begins to dig. His style is large, operatic: big strokes, very slowly made. He doesn't seem to be turning up many worms. "He's way inside," the angry man says.

"It's Binky Farmer," my guide says. "He's seventy-seven years old, that one."

"Way inside," the angry one repeats, but no one else seems to want to indict old Binky, whose only pension is a tide a day.

"Shoot him," the angry one says. "I mean it. Shoot him. It's the ethics of the thing."

My guide says, "It's not Binky who should be shot. It's these schoolteachers who come along in summah, trying to strike it rich during their taxpayer *vacation*."

All the boys turn subtly. Binky's off the spot. I'm back on. They eye me closely.

I pull out my pen, my little notebook, write down chunks of conversation to remind everyone what I'm here for.

My guide looks on curiously, but no way he'll penetrate my handwriting. He offers a quote, is visibly pleased when I write it down: "We'll all need boats before long with all these no-trespassing signs."

"Fucking summer dinks," says the angry one. "Just try to keep me off this fucking point!" He swipes his rake at the air. "I been coming out here since I was *seven*." He swipes the rake in my direction again, for emphasis, ready to pop my summerdink skull, find the worm within.

We watch the tide. It's going nowhere at all.

Five more wormers come into the meadow. No greetings, just nods, men who've known each other a long time. The new fellows take note of a stranger's presence, remain utterly silent, drift off to watch the tide from their own lookouts around the point. The rest of us watch the bay, watch the sky, watch old Binky as he straightens up, rests; we watch the seagulls, watch the island out there, watch as Binky goes back to work.

Suddenly, no word said, they're all rolling up their sleeves. Suddenly, the tide is right. I can't find my indicator rock— suddenly there are a million rocks. The new guys are off and moving through the mud. The father-and-son team hike off across the meadow to the other side of the neck, disappear. I had hoped to work near them, in the warmth of their kindness. My guide and the angry fellow step over the seaweed-covered rocks and into the mud right in front of us. Resolutely I follow, uninvited. It may not be much of a tide, it may not be deep mud, but after a short twenty minutes, I'm stuck good.

The angry guy looks back, laughs, shouts something.

"What?" I shout.

"I said, You are a *queer!*"

"Leave him for the *tide,*" my guide shouts. The two of them are laughing, hard, moving away from me.

"What?" I shout.

"Mud eel bite your *homo dick* off!" says the angry guy.

"What?" I shout.

My guide: "He won't get but four cents for *that* worm!"

Hor, hor, hor, hor, hor.

I'm alone. I struggle, still sinking. I drop my notebook, reach for it, lose my pen. I thrash after the notebook, quickly exhausted, then lose my hat, lose my sunglasses. I don't want to lose my Orvis wading boots, but after a struggle, I do lose them, abandon them there in the mud, socks too. The notebook is the one thing I manage to recover, and with it stuffed in my shirt I crawl and slither and drag myself to a rock near shore, pull myself puffing up onto it, sit heavily, watch the wormers move out and away chopping at the mud, warmed to their work, no thought of me in their heads.

"Fucking *queers!*" I shout. I'm reaching for an insult they might mind.

But they can't hear me. They're already hundreds of yards away in the wind, which comes at my face.

"Fucking *winter dinks!*"

They don't even turn their heads.

I drag myself rock to rock through the mud and to shore and slog my way back up the point through the yard of the summer mansion. All the no-trespassing signs have been torn down, torn to bits by those fellows who came after, strewn in bits everywhere along the way as if by some furious wind.

✧

Dicky Butts's wife drives the town school bus, part time. Health insurance? No way. Pension plan? Ha. They live in town, a quiet and genuine Maine place, a working town—no stores, no tourist facilities—just a village made of houses and trailers and shacks and sheds. Dicky's good little house is neatly kept, painted blue, on a small piece of an old family lot. His grandmother lives nearby, and his sister too, and his mom and dad, and his aunts and uncles and cousins and many a good friend. Their propinquity is his security, his insurance, his retirement plan.

Truey's house is on a corner of the property down by the road, next turn up from the worm shed. It's a small place, a ranch house, bedrooms in the basement. In the yard he's got an old army truck rebuilt to serve as a log skidder, huge tires draped with tractor chains—winter work. There are logs everywhere. Some cut, some tree length, all of them a season old, valuably waiting. Beside the skidder is his speedway trailer— high rack of worn racing slicks—leaning into the weather. The car itself, the estimable number five, is in a homebuilt garage, and in the garage is where you'll find Truey and Dicky, most high tides, mired in oil, changing engines, packing bearings, knocking out dents (of which in number five there are always plenty). Behind the garage in tall grass are a couple of car bodies—what's left of wrecks Truman and Dicky have used as parts for the racer. And there's kid stuff for the little boys— plenty of toys, a swing set, a play pool. Truey's wife is a nurse at the hospital in Calais, fifteen miles down Route 1. Her job provides the family with health insurance and a retirement plan. Her job also gives insurance of another kind: proof against bad worming.

Delores and Walter's house is at the top of a long, narrow lawn, a couple of football fields up the hill from the road and the worm shed. It's newish, set back on the hill, modern lines, tall windows, peaked ceiling, furniture-showroom furniture.

It's all very tidy, with an entire wall devoted to a wallpaper mountain scene, anything but the ocean.

It's well known, according to Walter, well known around the flats Downeast, that Delores runs the Walter Lock Jr. Bait Company. He means he's damn proud of her business acumen, and not afraid to say so. Delores is tanned and short and built delicately around the ankles and knees, bigger and sturdier on top. She wears large, round eyeglasses, gives an occasional smile, looks closely at you as you speak, her bullshit detector set on stun. Walter says she's tough—she's the one to sell something—sell a car, sell a house, sell the worms ("If these senators up in Washington was just women," he says again, has said it five or six times since I've known him). There's a sign in her handsome handwriting in the worm shed: "No more short counts. There will be no warning." I know it's her handwriting, because she's written me at the university, inviting me to come on back down, see the business end of things. It's her sense that I didn't quite get what I needed from the men, she wrote, in so many words, quite a few words. And today she's gone out of her way to answer all my questions, even suggesting questions to ask. She knows I want some color for my write-up (she calls it), so she has told me that she and Walter tried a couple of winters in Florida, picking oranges (piecework, like worms), but lately it's been back to year-round Maine. As for Truey, Truey may seem like a tough guy, but Truey is her little love bunny.

While Walter and Truey are out on the flats, she's on the phone and watching the fax—getting orders from distributors and retailers all over, filling them. She shows me how everything works. Charts and graphs and order sheets. The volume of her sales gets translated into limits: if she's got orders for 10,000 bloodworms and 5,000 sandworms on a given day, that's as many as she'll buy from her diggers. A 500-worm limit means a digger can make no more than $50.00 that day, no matter how prolific the mud. Some families, the ones Delores likes, can get around the limits by bringing spouses and sons and daughters into the picture.

In the worming shed—the windowless cinderblock basement of a truck garage (the garage now converted to an apartment—the days when they could afford to run their own trucks are over)—she washes the counting trays, packs the worms. She hasn't stopped moving since I arrived. The worms go in the usual cardboard flats for the distributors, 125 sands or 250 bloods in a bed of seaweed. Also, increasingly, Delores makes a special fisherman's ten-pack for bait shops to sell, her own invention. A little maiden-hair seaweed, ten carefully counted worms to a small, clear, plastic bag, a twist tie, then into a partitioned shipping box, cardboard lined with styrofoam:

LIVE SEA WORMS. RUSH!

A lot of work, something she didn't have to do in the past.

It's impossible to talk to her when she's counting; she doesn't hear or see, waits till the little bag she's working on is completely and neatly packed. She doesn't move quickly, even though it's familiar work; rather, she's elegant with it, as if she were cooking a fancy French dish. Between ten-packs she gives a small shrug, a smile, talks a snippet of politics, a bit of worm theory, tells a quick story, offers a confession: "Back when we were paying two and three cents a worm I'd kill 'em when they stung me. Now we're paying ten, I just pack the biters in like the rest." She likes her diggers loyal, she says, doesn't appreciate someone who's over limit trying to sell to other dealers, though she'll buy spare worms from almost anybody if she's got the orders.

Delores has two years of college, University of Southern Maine, thirty-some years back, cannot remember what major, did not get the degree. At this, I just shrug. For that, she likes me more. And I like her. She knows exactly who I am. She keeps me at her side, introduces me to everyone as a *scientist*. I don't correct her, and in some weird way my actual physical *stance* changes. The look on my face feels *scientific*. Even my questions change. I'm a new man. Give me a lab coat. I peer at the worms a whole new way, as if through some delicate instrument. For the first time among wormers I don't feel like an idiot. That's Delores.

In the hours after the tide the wormers come in, quietly, tiredly, make their counts. There's no banter, no conversation, no braggadocio. The diggers just come in. There's Jordon

LeMieux, whom Walter has called an ace blood digger. There's Spooky Nick, another ace, and Clarissa Larssen—the best woman wormer in Maine, in Walter's estimation. Squeak Snodgras comes in and counts his worms wordlessly, hands in his count slip, wordlessly leaves. There's a cool-looking teen boy, a hottie—Nike Air sneakers, t-shirt that says Slam Dunk, inner-city haircut—standing by his long-haired and tattooed dad, and in the counting room at prom time the boy is attentive, engaged, watches carefully as Pop counts his allowance worm by worm into the tray. Another father stands beside his daughter, an athletic and serious young woman of sixteen—very, very pretty—with mud to her eyelashes. They count. No one talks, not even all the young guys—a dozen of them in their twenties (their muddy pants low on their hips, showing the cracks of their fannies: wormer's cleavage). No chatter. No high fives. Nothing but the counting, the exchanging of slips, this scientist watching. There are two guys with ponytails like mine (that is, scraggly), a bunch with tattoos, several apparent bodybuilders, a thin fellow with Jesus Loves You on his sweatshirt. The wormers straggle in for a couple of hours, dumping their worms, counting them fast under fluorescent light, filling out their slips, collecting their cash or watching Delores put their counts in her book for a paycheck at the end of the week.

In a couple of months some of the boys will have to start blueberry picking up on the highlands; a few weeks past that some will go off logging. Some have skills like welding for whoever comes needing it; some will clean houses or leave town with construction crews or take temporary work at a mill. In December there's firewood chopping, even knickknack carving, and many an individual scheme. Then the new year: time to start thinking about the mud. Some guys will have to get out there in January—break the ice, dig the worms. Some will luxuriate till February. Some—the diggers with luck, or skills that match this year's needs, or spouses who work good jobs—some won't have to go out till March.

My first trip with the Downeast boys proved a good one for them, Walter and Dicky both counting 1500 sands—$90.00 each, plus enough bloods to carry the take over a hundred dollars for the tide. Truey, always a little more aggressive, got

1650 sands that day. Dicky was kind enough to count my worms for me, and after culling me about fifty (too small, or diseased, or broken by the bloods I'd thrown in with them), my count for the tide was an unspectacular 155 worms. $9.30. The five killer bloods in there brought my payday up to $9.80. I refused the cash, but Delores refused my refusal, and so—after a spot of negotiating, and a suggestion by Dicky—I became a minor sponsor of Truey's big number five, glory of the Bangor Speedway.

Still trying, I make yet another worming trip, drive down from Farmington the night before a tide Truey thinks'll be a good one, eat a diner dinner, stay at the Blueberry Motel. It's a nice late low tide, and I sleep in, eat a big breakfast. Truey's broken a camshaft in the race Saturday night and wrecked his engine, so there's extra incentive for a big day for all of us. My boots are tight; I've been out on my own in the mud below Milbridge, practicing. I've bought myself a sandworm hoe. I have my own gloves, a proper shirt. I know the Harrington River mud, now, and the Harrington River mud knows me. I'm ready to leave the ranks of professors, even scientists, ready to move up to shitdigger. The day is auspicious, the parking lot at Ripley Neck entirely full. Walter points out a Garney across the way, hovering in a workboat. "Spyglass," he says. "He'll sit there and wait to see where the real wormers go."

We cross the bay in good weather. The talk is briefly of cranberries: Walter has had a brainstorm: he'll dig a homemade bog in the woods up behind his house, grow cranberries. Dicky and Truey don't have much to say about that; then Truey invokes sea urchins, and they're off on that good subject again. $2800 a day, and you can go all winter. $2800 a day, and you don't have to worry about the worm market drying up, and you don't have to cut wood, or make wreaths, or shovel snow or work blueberries. You just get in your diving gear, bring up the urchins, get your body heat back in the hot tank on the deck of your boat, dive and dive and dive again, get rich on the Japanese.

"It's a hard winter in this county," as Walter says. Here in June, the Downeast boys are already thinking about ice.

That fucking spyglass Garney is going ashore in the neighborhood of some Milbridge boys. The sun is hot. Thunderheads are building up. You think of lightning, then you think of yourself plugged into the mud, the highest thing for hundreds of yards around, a lightning rod. Workboats are tooling every which way, and Truey and Dicky and Walter know everyone. "That fellow there is Minton Frawley. He went out to Arizona one winter and got himself in the movies. Did you see *Stir Crazy?* He's the guy looking up the girl's crotch in that bar scene."

"He's back worming," Dicky says.

"Scared of lightning," Truey says, meaning Frawley. "He'll run at the first boom-boom. Watch him."

"Winter does take a toll," Walter says, drifting on his own raft of thought. When we hit the mud, Walter gets in it, immediately marches to a big mussel flat and begins to dig its borders. Dicky and Truey and I wait. Like most wormers, they like to watch the tide, size it up, have a chat. "Ask your daddy how many orders he's got," Dicky says. "I need some ambition."

He does look tired.

Truey just watches his father at work.

Dicky sizes up the tide, pretends a discouragement that looks real: "I don't think this is going to be a profitable day, Truey."

My deadline is long gone, my story's a kill, but here I am. The guys don't pay much attention to me anymore, negative or positive. I'm up to about forty bucks in Truey's race car. Maybe one Saturday soon I'll go to the races, hang in the pit, a scientist, see, interested in speed. Maybe *Harper's* will like that story!

There's a rumble of thunder, not far distant. Truey smiles briefly at Dicky's joking, goes over the gunwales, gets himself ready to worm. Dicky reluctantly follows. I'm so reluctant I just sit in the boat and watch them start. More thunder.

"There he goes," Truey says. Sure enough, movie-star Frawley has turned his boat around and is heading back in.

Truey takes his shirt off, and you have to wonder if his naked-lady tattoo is by the same artist as Dicky's. It's the same woman, same colors, same thick lines. I climb into the mud. Today I plan to up my sponsorship of the glorious number five to serious partnership proportions. Today I want to dig like a Downeast boy.

Truey is already at it, working hard.

Dicky can't seem to get started. "Help," he says. A plaintive joke. He doesn't feel like it today. In the end, though, he'll get 1900 sandworms, 120 bloods: $126.00, a super tide. Truey will get 2100 sands, fifty bloods. A money tide, a monster. Walter will do as well as Dicky. I will get 210 sandworms, zero bloods, working hard as I've ever worked, chopping and stomping and picking, legs sore as hell from previous outings, shoulders aching, mind blank, struggling in the mud, turning it, panting, mucking along, pulling worms: $12.60.

Truey hikes off far away across the mud. Later, when the tide comes up, we'll have to go pick him up. Walter is chopping away at some distant mussel mound. Dicky doesn't range too far, gradually gets his rhythm, digs faster and faster, coming into the worms. I never get a rhythm at all, stay close to the boat, trying to get a whole tide in, no breaks, no getting stuck. I know how to walk now, don't pause long enough to sink, but march forward, ever forward, chop left, chop middle, chop right, pulling worms from the mud. To me, they seem scarce today. To me, they seem terribly fragile. I break every third worm, miss a million that zip into their holes before I can get hold. The thunder booms a little closer.

Late in the tide, Dicky starts saying "Help," again, just kind of saying it out loud every twenty steps or so, groaning comically. He's found some good mud, is plunking worms into his box three and four at a dig. "Help," he moans, kidding around. Then he shouts: "Truey, let's quit." It's an old joke, and from across the flat Truman Lock gives Dicky the finger. Dicky excavates his way through the mud, pulling worms, pulling worms, dunking them in his box, saying "Help, Truey. Truey, help," a mantra for the dig. Then he bellows, loud as hell across the mud: *Truey, get me outta here* and then he shouts it again.

You Have Given
This Boy Life

When I have kids, friends told me, it would get worse, this intermittent death thing of mine (priest to his parents at Jimmy Passaro's baptism: "You have given this boy life, but you have also given him death"). For now, it comes and goes predictably with the other rites of passage. My wedding, Jesus: ghosts everywhere, but that was years back. Then the big job change, from the University of Maine at Farmington to Ohio State, and with that the big move, and the toggling back and forth: summers in Maine, school year in Ohio, the movement of seasons and years delineated by the long car trip, packed boxes, hellos, good-byes. And then, surprise, middle age. I came to Ohio on the old side of young. But suddenly, no. I can very nearly point to the day the change came. Eyeglasses, for one thing. A student calling me Dad by mistake. And then, tenure and promotion at that great and eternal Midwestern land-grant university. I celebrated with the others who didn't get fired, but I was unaccountably depressed. Options seemed to narrow. Where once there had been the whole world to live in on the whim of choice, there was now . . . Ohio. Glum, glum, congratulations, Bill! Grim, grim, the march is on. Unanimous vote! You are in!

You're going to die.

Behind our rented house in Columbus ("Poor, gray Columbus," young Robert Lowell mourned in a letter home), the leaves fell and revealed neighbors' yards and also a large parking lot that happily I mistook when it was wet for a black pond. Often it was wet that winter, often the lot was water, only a rare police car, idling, to kill the illusion. Empty, empty.

But suddenly, the lot would be full for a few odd days, then empty again for several more, then—around Christmas—full for weeks, then empty and full sporadically all the way into spring. One influx would be rich: Mercedes, Jaguars, Cadillacs. The next a different class altogether: pickups, muffler draggers, rusty old American sedans, low to the ground, shocks dead. The next, family values: minivans, "sport utility" vehicles (to me, these look like running shoes), Volvo wagons. Always there was a thread of some kind in the grouping of autos. A puzzle, that lot, the kind of thing I notice while shouting blues songs and crashing live riffs on the piano, looking out the window as if into a huge crowd at Woodstock, rainy morning: fantasy.

I didn't figure it out till I saw the hearse one day: the O.O. Olson funeral home out on High Street. Of course. What must Olson's full name be? Oscar Oliver? Anyway, his initials are O.O.O. His monogrammed towels, his ring, imagine: oOo.

For five years or more after in dreams I saw the young man's Nike Air sneakers, and the puddle he lay in, and the dark square of sky at the top of the air shaft. The dreams focus on his chest somehow, his perfect chest exposed so fast by the ALS guys, his bright brown skin, his beauty, his youthful belly, the band of his boxers, his one moan as the medics sought his wounds, which were many, and not only from the fall. The dream is static, no movement, a vision really—dying boy, odiferous air shaft, cops, a certain hovering viewpoint—fixed, everlasting.

At a dinner party in SoHo, lower Manhattan, I got seated at the very end of a long table next to Larry Vignoble, the mysterious new boyfriend of an actress I knew back then. Across the table perched an intent woman I didn't know at all. The guy to my left was enormous and sat with his back turned, effectively isolating me from the rest of the party. Beside the intent woman was a nervous young actor with a long chin and judgmental eyes. He stared down at the head of the table, seeming to hope he was finally in the presence of his big break (and maybe he was). I guess I hoped the same most days in New York.

As we ate the salad thrust over our shoulders by catering staff, the woman and Larry Vignoble and I began to chat, even grew voluble, and it seemed less to matter that the famous people I'd come hoping to meet were far up the line of faces by the host, talking, clinking, laughing hard. My interlocutors and I got past the weird weather of that season and dismissed the Mets and Yankees easily, then the lady told us what she did: public relations. What do *you* do? she asked me. I saw that she hoped I was famous, or at least important. I didn't want to talk about what I did because what I did in those days amounted to nothing, in most people's eyes. I tried to put a good face on it, said I was a contractor, said I was a writer. Trying to be a writer, was the exact phrase. I could have said trying to be a contractor, too.

The big man next to me turned at that, smiled indulgently. "You'll get there," he said. Then quite subtly and charmingly he turned the talk at our end of the table to his scriptwriting successes. People several seats down began to listen. He was hilarious and quick and likeable and had big names rolling from his lips: Dusty, Meryl, Madonna. He included me with winks and pats on the hand. He graciously declined to talk about money when someone asked, and—just when the time was right, just when you felt he was dominating the talk—he handed the baton to Larry Vignoble: And what about you?

You could see Larry wasn't in the mood to talk about what he did any more than I had been. But everyone at our end of the table had fallen silent, regarded him benignly. He shrugged and said, "I work in Jersey." Still the expectant silence. "For a small company," he said.

"What company?" said the PR lady, with the air of a person who knows all companies large and small.

"What sort of work?" said the scriptwriter.

Larry gave a sad smile, said, "I am a funeral director."

The answers to two or three questions from the scriptwriter made it clear: a funeral director is an undertaker, a mortician, an embalmer, haberdasher to the deceased, makeup on dead skin, barrels of loose body parts, ghosts, death, doom, horror, despair.

Deep pause.

The scriptwriter said, "Well."

We turned to the nervous, good-looking fellow, who smiled painfully and started to talk about the class he was taking with Uta Hagen at the Actor's Studio.

But quickly some uproar at the host's end got the scriptwriter shouting wittily, the PR lady laughing. Both of them turned to the length of the table, silencing the young actor, cutting the mortician and me off entirely from everyone but one another.

I turned to Larry, said, "All right," meaning that his work interested me. We drank sips of wine.

He said, "It's a job," understanding what I'd meant.

I asked how he'd learned his trade. I mean, how did someone learn that stuff?

He said that, okay, a lot of morticians grew up in a family trade. But some didn't. He hadn't. "Christ, my dad's an engineer at WABC radio." He eyed me suspiciously, trying to know whether my interest was real. He seemed to see it was, seemed to trust me not to make any jokes. He let it out: he'd gone to the Cincinnati College of Mortuary.

I said I knew at dental schools they practiced on plaster heads and porcelain teeth, hoping to lead him along.

He said at mortuary school they practiced on dummies, first. Then cadavers. Then actual newlydeads (he said) whose families got the benefit of a budget funeral. But the general public doesn't think past the dead-body stuff. Part of the curriculum at school, for example, was a psychology course about grief. And you took business courses: bookkeeping, marketing, advertising. You took medical courses: anatomy, communicable diseases, embalming.

The party carried on up table, but Larry and I talked. He was glad of my interest, said people seldom wanted to talk about what he did except to accuse the trade of deception, chicanery, dishonesty. This brought the blood to his cheeks. He sipped wine, looked up-table at his girlfriend by the host. At length he said that somehow he'd been drawn to funeral practices from high school. Did all his papers on subjects of death: Amish burial practices, say, or treatment of the dead in Homer's *Iliad*. Couldn't say why. Something about the quiet dignity of the enterprise, its plain necessity. Also, he'd been curious, drawn to the dead.

After mortician school he'd lucked out and gotten this job in Jersey right away. Super benefits. Fair pay. And there were quite a few weeks in the year with no work, since people tend to die in bunches. Stedler Funeral Home averaged seventy funerals a year, most in the winter, a lot toward the end of summer, not many in the spring or fall.

I found a roundabout way to ask if he thought he'd gotten inured to death. He said, "No way. Nope. In fact, doing that work is really, really scary. You just can't *believe* all the ways there are to die."

𝒟

My dad took us five Roorbach kids to Jones Beach on Long Island, New York, once or twice a summer to get our early sixties sunburns and to get smashed up in the real surf and to have a day of it, a long ride from Connecticut. In the car we all called first shower (you sang it loud: *I call first shower*) and felt itchy with the salt and roasted by the sun, burned to a crisp. I see even now the traffic jams there, and then a particular jam, the cars just stopped in thick air. Ahead you could see police lights, hear the sirens coming.

"Accident," Dad said sighing.

Then our lane began to move, bumps and starts, bringing us closer to the flashing lights, the trouble. On a bridge over an inlet the road was mostly blocked with police cars and fire engines, men milling about, an ambulance, a guy out of uniform directing traffic through the breakdown lane one car at a time. Down in the marsh reeds four cops leaned dolefully, their heads almost touching, looking at something. Dad moved a slow car-length ahead, and I saw the heart of things: a motorcycle seriously mangled, partly hanging off the bridge. On the sidewalk a teenage girl in a bikini lay on her back with her head crushed badly and the cops and two doctors (yes, doctors then, straight to the tragedy, no EMTs or ALS in between) busy around her.

Pop said, "Don't look," but we did. We looked, knowing we should not, that we were rude to look, or worse. Our station wagon idled. We'd been halted by the plainclothesman's hand; the ambulance was maneuvering. What else could we do? The girl's lips moved like talking, but she was not talking. She put a hand to her face, let the hand drop, felt the pavement beside her. Then she died. You saw the life leave her, somehow. You saw how it couldn't stay. I knew what I had seen. The doctors saw it too, looked at each other, looked sick, really, looked at one another helplessly, stopped their ministrations in the hot white sunlight. One of the cops brought a blanket.

I looked till suddenly the plainclothesman waved and Pop hit the gas and we were free. He said, "That was awful to see." And he said something grim about motorcycles. He also used the word rubberneckers with some disgust, and defined it for us: people who slow down to look at these things, people who clearly weren't us.

Pretty soon being kids we were nuts again and calling first showers and saying how we would kill each other. Pop was quiet, quiet the whole ride home. But later, when I couldn't sleep from the sunburn, later I just lay there in my bed thinking about that girl. That older kid in her bikini. Dying and then dead. When a minute before she'd just been riding along behind her boyfriend, maybe laughing, holding his flat stomach. The whole thing had a kind of plainness to it: if your head got crushed, you died, just like anything that got its head crushed, just like anything, a squirrel or an ant or a dog.

And even in my wildest high school and college years I never took the slightest interest in motorcycles—stayed away from them, in fact.

I kept calling Larry Vignoble because I wanted to do a story on his work. I wanted to do a story on his work because I was morbidly interested in his work. I mean, it was morbid work, and that was exactly why I'd got so interested. I called him a couple of times, trying to interest him in my interest, in the supposed interest my readers would have, that some important magazine would have. But I'd had something of a breakthrough: for the first time I was more interested in my subject than in venal and unwriterly ambition. I wanted to see the whole death operation, from pickup to burial. I wanted to see an embalming. I wanted a tour of the morgue.

"No way," Larry said. "I've got to protect people's privacy. That's the main part of my work."

"They're dead," I said. "What privacy?"

"The families aren't dead," he said. "Think about it. Your wife, say."

"I'm not married," I said, though in two months I would be and actually could see his point.

"Then think about your mother there," he said. "You want everybody looking at your mother dead and naked and all fucked up?"

On Martha's Vineyard I went to nude beaches with my friends and got sunburned like a little kid. I'd lie in the sand with my naked white butt in the air and cook it so badly you'd think I had red underpants on. And we friends would swim and nap away hangovers and flirt politely with naked young women and turn handsprings into the surf and yell with laughter and with being alive and having nothing better to do but feel the sand and be with young women and not think of the future (except maybe the coming sundown, or even on a bad day as far ahead as fall).

The best beach was Zack's at that time, up-island below the cliffs on Gay Head. At Zack's there were few older folks and few folks in any case and a guy who flew in from Boston in his private helicopter and a Korean woman with a surfboard and a muscular black man who juggled and a pair of white sisters who sat lotus back to back. The cliffs were made of clay in many colors and every day naked people bathed in the clay and walked the beach covered in it, prehistoric souls. Some were tourists, some were islanders, some were like us: young and willing to be poor and to take sporadic work—just enough work so we could manage a whole summer loafing.

We went to Lucy Vincent Beach too, which is the town beach of Chilmark. To get on that strand you needed to know someone from Chilmark, or hitchhike in with a stickered car. There were other scams, too: phony leases, altered passes, friends at inns, even counterfeit car stickers. We were alive. And each summer we'd find the way to get on that beach. At Lucy Vincent you'd walk a half mile down the sand to get to the clothes-optional area, a few hundred yards of exquisite sand and dunes and real surf and rocks.

There we sat amidst families: kids trying handstands, coolers and sandwiches, volleyball, sand castles. Rich families. Mercedes and Volvos in the small parking lot, movie-star sightings, attorneys general, surgeons, successful artists: everyone naked. We met psychiatrists and architects and writers for the *New York Times;* we met professors and construction bosses and the mayor of New Haven, Connecticut. We met their daughters, too, and liked them or even loved them, got over, got rejected, got over that, got over with someone else.

And one day a corpulent old guy was playing in the surf, really having a blast, yelling with laughter like a hatchling, kicking the waves, watching the young women, holding his arms out wide to accept the horizon, swimming, floating, bodysurfing, inspecting shells, diving. Displacing more water than most men, he dove and romped in the sea, then trotted pinkly up the beach. We noticed him and his happiness, his big, important nakedness. His vacation must have just started. Late in the day he stood up to his waist in the water and gazed out at the great Atlantic. When a big wave broke, he let out a yell and dove under it, then surfaced and stood and watched the sea, and shouted and dove, and stood and watched, dripping, grinning. Then he fell. I saw him fall; quite a different gesture from the dives. Bolt of lightning. No dramatic hand to the chest, nothing like that. He just dropped face first into the water and did not get up. Too slowly I got myself up off my towel and ran down to the water and with several naked souls who had also seen him collapse dragged him up out of the foam and onto wet sand. He was not alive. I knew this from experience of the living; something we apprehend in the air around one another was missing, something the presence of which is only confirmed when gone, maybe electrical impulses, maybe something more holy, I don't know. Or maybe it was nothing, just emotion, the romance I attached to all experience at that age.

On the rich beach there happened to be three doctors in three separate family groups, and the three, two women and a man, rushed to the fat burgher and went to work. One, prepared for anything and not afraid of lawyers, even had his black bag along. All were naked: extinct patient, three doctors, those who would help them, those who could only watch—all the rest of us. A man known for his determined jogging put a towel around his waist and ran off, a mile plus to tell the gate guard to call the police.

On the beach one of the doctors had taken charge and CPR was in progress, but not simple CPR: some kind of doctor's CPR, one naked man puffing breaths into another's gaping mouth, one naked woman lifting the patient's thick naked legs high in the air, one naked observer pumping the man's dead chest, the last naked doctor injecting adrenaline, saying calm instructions. How fat the dead man was. How dead he was. How dedicated the doctors were despite this.

At length, the Chilmark Police Department beach Bronco arrived, and two dressed people—police officers—helped lift the great man onto a stretcher, helped put him in the car, and, never flagging with the CPR, two of the doctors climbed in naked beside him, continuing their hopeless work. They all drove away and the beach was itself again: the tide rising to cover the small marks the man's plight had made in the sand; the children returning to their games; the adults turning inward; the young adults—my friends, me—turning to excited and respectful analysis of the event we'd witnessed.

The police came back to get an ID, but no one knew the guy. We knew he'd been sitting approximately there, somewhere over there. The cops waited and as people left the beach in the lateness of the afternoon a little pile of clothing gained prominence, and there in some white shorts was a wallet, and the dead man had a name.

We friends agreed over many beers that night that the whole thing was pretty cool: the guy came into the world naked and wet and alone, and he left it so, and left it happy, with maybe only one last blast of fear. Lovely, idyllic, we said. But we were young.

⸎

Larry Vignoble wouldn't talk to me anymore. I'd been calling him once a week, trying different stratagems. I wanted access to that embalming room. He'd become suspicious. But this wasn't sick. I wanted to see if I could figure out what the body means without a soul (if that's what is missing, finally), or see what the body doesn't mean. I was about to get married and I was suddenly thirty-six years old and for the first time I really knew something: living doesn't last. I wanted to look this death thing straight in the face. I wanted to see Larry sewing lips shut or repairing the damage to a face from a fall. From this I was sure I would learn something important, something that would extend my understanding of life and of being alive and ease my new worries about the speed of time.

I went to the New York City Library and took out old books: *Death Customs*, by E. Bendann, written in 1930: "The Vedic Hindu when cremating their dead cried out 'Away, go away, O Death!'" and "It is a custom of the Fiji Islands to break down the side of the house to carry out a dead body, although the door is wide enough" and "In Savo, the bodies of commoners are thrown into the sea . . ." I got out *On Death and Dying*, by Elisabeth Kübler-Ross (she of the famous five stages of grief), thought with her prompting about how strictly death these days has been quarantined, denied, made invisible. We don't get to see it much, not the way our grandparents did, or mine, anyway, born at the end of the nineteenth century, Victorian times, when six of ten infants didn't make it to adulthood. And people conceived ten children in those days because they were aware of those kind of odds. My mother's mother watched several siblings die. My mother, one of eight kids, saw her older brother Bobby die of polio at five. My own four siblings and I have all made it to adulthood, all five of us, unscathed. What with modern medicine and pasteurized foods we didn't have to think about dying at all. Death was not in our house. You could forget about death.

I read and I read more, twenty books with Death in their titles. I didn't even know what I was looking for. Comfort? A reprieve? What on earth good was reading going to do?

I read *The American Way of Death,* by Jessica Mitford, and suddenly understood Larry Vignoble's defensiveness. It's she who exposed abusive practices—the switching of coffins, impossible promises, the preying on bereavement—back in the fifties. All of which led to laws, regulations, associations of ethical practitioners, but also to a lasting negative impression of the undertaking trade, which trade didn't exactly need bad press to begin with. If you were in funerary service (as Larry called it), you didn't want a reporter in there even if you never did anything wrong, because no matter what you did your work was death and you were an emblem of death and would always be unwelcome, unclean, a ghoul with formaldehyde faintly on your breath, your fingers stained. I called Larry and mentioned the Mitford book. He *freaked*. "I fucking *knew* it," he said. He'd read Mitford, all right. All the funeral directors I talked to in those months had, some of them five times. Mention Jessica Mitford to a funeral director if you want to get below that famous layer of reserve.

I read Martin Buber on death, Dostoyevski, Heidegger. I asked friends for theories and experiences till they told me to shut up. I talked to peaceful old people, those who were or pretended to be resigned, but if you didn't believe much in the Judeo-Christian God what they said was useless. I comforted myself with what a biology professor had told us in college: that people are matter, that matter cannot be destroyed, that every molecule goes back into the soil or into the air or out into the infinite Universe and gets reused somewhere and soon. Even as the freshman I was, I saw this recycling as reincarnation, and believed. It's comforting: you will come back as everything, always, and you were always everything before. Death is a matter of thermodynamics: all matter seeks randomness. Life is only a temporary bid against entropy, a temporary organization of molecules by a force which is life. I re-read Kurt Vonnegut, *Slaughterhouse Five,* wherein the Tralfamadorians faraway on a distant planet say, "So it goes," whenever they hear of a death.

Your grandmother is dead? So it goes. They can also see time, all time at once, and know that one's death has always happened, and always will.

I was thirty-six and for the first time I couldn't throw a baseball more than twice from the outfield without pain, couldn't run indefinitely or even reliably, couldn't drink hard without paying dearly, couldn't miss sleep gracefully. The change was pronounced and sudden. In the decade plus that has disappeared since then I've gotten used to this new, more frail (if larger) body. I'm in a less athletic phase, that's all. Life comes in stages. Or should I say that other word?

In my late twenties in Greenwich Village I went to bars nightly, either playing music or listening to it. Preacher's was in a basement on Bleecker Street, and there a man called the Preacher, a former priest, provided live music and sold drinks to the living (he had a photo of himself in vestments next to the cash register, and under that a message for the bartenders: Thou Shalt Not Steal). He was fair to the musicians and calm and didn't judge anybody at all.

One spring night I went there to see a friend perform, a lady with a big voice and big good looks and a lot of showy, hilarious personality. She wore a shiny silver shirt that showed her navel. She wore a skirt and under the skirt silver underpants you saw repeatedly. She sang Aretha Franklin songs and Bonnie Raitt songs and gospel stuff, and she was *hot*.

On her break she sat with us at our table and we barked and roared with laughter and told her how her singing knocked us *out*. We felt good being her friends, joked all the louder for being noticed with her, admired her as she fielded compliments from a virtual receiving line of strangers, the Preacher's other customers, scores of them, red-faced, sweaty from dancing, relieved for the moment of unhappiness.

A little fellow walked up, nicely glazed, and over the loud jukebox yelled how wonderful our friend was, how wonderful and how beautiful, and in her joy at possessing these talents

Shermaze (I will call her Shermaze) leapt up and began to dance in place, shaking her ample, vital body under her tight silver bodice, and we laughed and the little man laughed and danced and you knew he hadn't had a woman smile at him in a very long time. He grew more excited, and more red in the face, shouted "Hey!" and danced, and Shermaze (not making fun, and not afraid to be a fool, and not afraid he'd misunderstand), Shermaze shouted back and danced harder, looking into his eyes, shouting *Honey!*

The man fell across the table, never losing the big smile, fell directly on our table. Quickly the ambulances came and the EMS guys and ALS, but by now you know the theme of this little catalogue of mine and have guessed: our man was dead. Poor Shermaze; she blames herself still.

My gorgeous niece Kristen when she was four (a long, long time ago, but quick, seventeen years), always asked if she could see what I had under any Band-Aids. She liked me particularly in this regard because I was doing a lot of plumbing and tiling work then and always had terrible cuts on my hands and was willing to show her. She'd say, "Can I see?" And I'd peel off the bandage. She'd study the cut or bruise or blister steadfastly—this tiny little girl—study this evidence of my fragility until she'd had enough and went to get me a fresh bandage.

People gather around. In primitive cultures without shame, in the more repressed (our own, right now, though TV changes this), furtively. People gather to see. They gather to learn something. Rubbernecking is a tool of survival. You look a long time so you can learn: What was the exact error here?

I sold my death story idea to *7 Days*, a big, beautiful weekly magazine in New York. The editor came up with a structure for me: A Day in the Life of Death. I did the preliminary work with real excitement. I was going to be a writer if it killed me. Poor Larry Vignoble, harassed by me past all sympathy, wouldn't take my calls. But I had to have a funeral home. I called all the mortuaries in New York City, trying to line people up. Everyone I talked to was suspicious. No funeral director would talk to me, much less show me anything, even though I told them I wasn't Jessica Mitford. They knew that name, all right, banged phones down when I intoned it. In desperation I posed as the nephew of a dying society matron, got to see the most expensive coffins in New York City ($175,000), purported guiltily to ask questions as my aunt's advisor: How long would her remains last? (No guarantees.) Was a woman embalmer available? (But of course.) Would they have to cut her favorite dress to get it on her? (Possibly, though rigor slackens as the days after death pass.) Would they have to sew her lips shut? The funeral director was somber and all business, honest and straightforward as death itself. "No sewing," he said. (I learned later that the modern trade uses Crazy Glue, and sweetheart, those lips stay shut.)

Finally, I found a convivial mortician in the Bronx who believed in openness. He even used the term *glasnost* when we spoke. He'd show me whatever I wanted to see, tell me whatever I wanted to know. In long interviews I heard about his childhood in the funeral business, his fear of AIDS, his stories of drugs smuggled in corpses. He told me the realities of racism even toward corpses, the industry attitude toward sex with cadavers (which with a wry grimace he called dead-sticking, and a sordid myth). For forty-five minutes he listed weird ways to die, one whole side of a tape: yeast infection of the blood, power drill through the head, space heater in the bathtub, untreated cut on the foot, tree limb in a windstorm, cue ball lodged in the esophagus, tooth infection, falls into elevator shafts, milking-machine masturbation, chunks of ice from building ledges, multitudinous adventures with alcohol, male violence, a hundred forms of suicide, plenty more, including 1001 diseases you never heard of. He complained of sloppy autopsies, sinking grave sites, lazy shovel men. He showed me his whole operation, from pickup to cleansing, from haircut to hole in the ground.

I lined up a date with the New York City Morgue, scheduled a shift with the New York City Emergency Medical Service (called EMS), got permission to visit two emergency rooms. Everybody everywhere was suspicious. They'd all been jerked around by reporters before. But they all wanted their pictures in the paper, their names in print, public confirmation of their lives.

My Day in the Life of Death turned out to be Good Friday. Also the thirteenth of April. Just a coincidence. I picked up a corpse at LaGuardia Airport at 6 a.m. with my Bronx pal, went on from there, straight through to midnight.

✐

Code 100, or something like that. A kid has been thrown off the roof of a building on 141st Street. The cops are there already. They walk us (medics, supervisor, nervous reporter) through a dripping archway into a basement-level air-shaft courtyard and there the boy lies. He makes noises like humming, breathing hard. The EMTs work on him and intently I watch. The cops watch, too, make jocular conversation, loudly ask what the fuck I think I'm going to learn from standing around in piss and puke.

He's an athletic kid, washboard stomach, muscled thighs, great biceps. This much you can see. You can't see how smart or dumb he is or how well loved; you can't see his kindnesses (if any), his crimes (if any), his girlfriend at home. He wears new Nike Air sneakers which the EMTs scissor off his feet. He lies in urine that is not his own. He hums. On my tape, you can actually hear his humming.

"Ah, crap, knife wound," one of the EMTs says suddenly. "Here too," says another, and puts his clean finger deep in the slit, trying to tell how deep.

The ALS guys duck in—Advanced Life Support—and calmly they go to work.

This boy who couldn't fly has been stabbed six times and thrown off a roof. He hums. I hear that humming now, even without the tape.

During a long ten minutes the medics get his neck immobilized and his blood-pressure pants in place and get him on a stretcher and into an ambulance. On the way into Harlem Hospital he suddenly sits up, opens his blank eyes, rips the IV from his arm, rips the oxygen mask from his face. Then he falls back, dead. I am right there, crouching.

Away! Go away, O Death!

I wrote the article, got it in on time; I forget which day in May, except that it was the same day *7 Days Magazine* folded. I felt bereft, guilty, as if my story had killed the magazine somehow. And as if the magazine's death might kill my supposedly budding journalism career. So it goes. But the story ended up elsewhere. *New York Magazine,* if you want to know. October 1990. No problem. "A Day in the Life of Death." Five in the morning to midnight, Good Friday. The only real trouble I had was that the hospital wouldn't verify the murdered boy's death. I don't blame them. Death looks bad. But because I couldn't verify, the fact checkers at *New York* wouldn't let me say it.

But here I will: he died. That kid died. I knew it then and I know it now. And I see his lean form and hear his humming when I least wish to. And no matter how many times I dream that dream I don't learn anything useful from him at all. Nothing. And nothing from the motorcycle crash or the fat man whose heart burst in spindrift or the little man who danced himself to death in the Preacher's busy bar, nothing at all from the half year of study and reporting that came later. What was I doing, anyway? What did I think I'd learn, staring at death so hard, so shamelessly?

Death exacts awe, it's true, and the awful demands a certain amount of looking away. Perhaps the looking away has something to do with the privacy Larry Vignoble kept talking about. And maybe such denial is a mistake, as Kübler-Ross says, a flaw of the modern Western character. But then again, isn't denial a survival tactic in itself? Why live with fate as with some depressed and depressing lover when there are girls in bikinis walking by and boys with flat stomachs?

Today a funeral in the rain at O.O. Olson's. I rock the piano and look out the window. Before long here the trees will bud and leaf and I won't see it so clearly anymore. Anyway. Someone rich—the lot is full of Mercedes parked in the rain on wet pavement as on the surface of some black pond.

Vortex

Mike and I, what can I say, we liked to fish. We might argue about music or compete over women, but fish, fish we could talk about that summer, especially bluefish. We'd climb in my truck and roar out to Squibnocket Beach five in the morning and fish with the tide. We'd get on the ferry to Chappaquiddick after a shaky gig in Edgartown and spend the night on the beach flinging lures and drinking hard and talking *fish,* if not catching them. We are both second brothers in families with three boys, for what that might be worth to you in understanding our troubled and blessed alliance. I'm ten years older than he, for what that might add. And this happy story is years ago, going on two decades, is set back when we'd known each other ten years already—I'd known him from a teen—back when time and place and whatever other hidden stuff hadn't intervened and let us drift apart.

Martha's Vineyard, late afternoon tide approaching. All day indoors practicing for a gig later in the week and we're both thinking about fishing, no matter how hard Adam hits the drums, no matter the chord changes Jon's calling out, no matter if our mouths are singing and our fingers are playing, no matter what, Mike and I are thinking fish.

And we're both low-key getting into my old truck when rehearsal is done. Our surf rods are already back in the bed of the bombish F-100 (since retired), where they do live. Our reels—representing our life savings—are on the rods. Our bait buckets are back there and our tackle boxes, such as they are. We say see-you-laters to the rest of the boys in the band, get in the truck just like going downtown—cool as wild cucumbers—we don't want a crowd coming with us today. Those other guys aren't serious. Those other guys—fuck 'em—will want to leave before the fish come in. Or they'll complain if there aren't any fish. They don't really know what we know, what fishing really is: that peaceful, soulful bump in your chest and your eyes watching the water. Afternoon tide is so nice and quiet, and you might catch a fish for the party at Robertini's tonight. You might. You don't know. We stop in Oak Bluffs for Bobby Robertini, who's also serious, but he says, "Nah." He's been on the island two weeks already and hasn't caught a fish, is losing his edge, we like to say. He's getting spoiled by the family boat. We don't make fun or press him, because more is not merrier, not in Lobsterville anyway.

We roar up-island, catching views out over the ocean, talking fish. I take the big right onto the Lobsterville road, fighting that wheel and changing those gears, and we cruise, watching that water. We've caught the tide. We've caught it all right! I park the bomb at Lobsterville, Lobsterville nothing but the end of a road across the inlet from Menemsha, which is a real fishing port, a genuine seaside village, beset by tourists, protected by money. But Lobstahville, Lobstahville is just a road ending in a steep ramp to deep water and signs saying *Road Ends Here* so drunken summer dinks and certain senators don't dunk their Caddies. There's a dock there and a few small boats from Gay Head but mostly dinghies floating in the little pond that makes a bit of harbor. But that's it. It's no *ville*.

And we're just slowly getting our tackle out—no rush—when we become aware of the gulls and terns wheeling in the sky over where the jetty would be. We spy that enormous cloud of terns and gulls and just grab our gear and run, two guys trundling over the dunes, two big guys, sunburned and freckled and unkempt, one in sneakers, one barefoot. The day is cool, high, heavy clouds in crisp blue, heavy wind, onshore. The Lobsterville jetty when we get there is empty but for one fisherman, and this one lone man is fighting a fish, his pole bent almost double. Whitecaps lash the rocks. Mike and I, oh Jesus, we run faster, struggling in the deep sand. Laughing gulls swoop and fall into the heavy chop around the head of the jetty, picking off baitfish. A cheering line of big herring gulls and black-backed gulls at water's edge, sated, throw their heads back, yelping and chortling continuously. The terns hover aloft, tireless, wheeling and diving, smacking the water, carrying off sand eels. My heart leaps in my chest.

Mike and I, we skip carelessly from boulder to boulder on the jetty, because suddenly we've seen the furious boiling of a great school of feeding bluefish and the frantic, churning, sometimes flying, escapes of schools of their prey: tinker mackerel, for sure. Sand eels, too. Flat-sided, flashing herring, like stainless steel brooches moving light speed through the very surface of the water.

"Everywhere!" the lone fisherman shouts in the wind. His cap says Martha's Vineyard in neat gold letters. He's lanky and kindly, a generous soul. He seems real glad to have folks to share his luck, and he talks oddly in excitement: "Bloody ding-dong everywhere!"

Mike and I, we hurry; the blues could be gone in an instant. High tide about to turn, the water rough, good breeze, whitecaps breaking over the jetty and washing our pants cuffs, the sun two hours from setting into the Elizabeth Islands, those big clouds shooting in the stratosphere, keeping their distance from each other, from the earth below. The world is all sound and light and splashing fish.

I impatiently watch my thick stupid hands push fourteen-pound monofilament through loops and turns, careful not to hurry and make a weak knot. When the steel leader is finally secure, I clip an orange plastic Atom on. I don't have a green-backed Atom to match the bait mackerel, but we are after bluefish, not stripers or bonito, and bluefish won't care.

Mike? Mike is already casting a Hopkins, a very simple dimpled chunk of flashing stainless steel with a hank of deer hair at the hook end. He barks, "I'm on!" the second his lure hits the water. His pole bends deeply, as the fish fights to stay where she is. Oh, Mike's pole bends and the line shoots out, reel singing, as the bluefish turns, dives, makes a run.

I fire my Atom out over the water. The Atom, a thick, buoyant cylinder of pressed polystyrene with two sets of treble hooks, imitates a wounded and struggling baitfish. I reel it in fast, jerking the rod tip to make the lure pop and jump and waggle. Almost immediately a bluefish appears behind it, catching up, breaking the water, all mouth and fins. I crank faster yet, as fast as I can, feeling something of the terror those tinker mackerel must feel, fleeing. The blue swims up beside the lure, turns his head, and with the slightest pause for inspection— slam!—hits it with a splashing, ice-cold leap and chomp. The fish turns now and sinks to carry its prize away. My long surf rod bends like it's made of grasses. The fish stops. I freeze. The two of us stay like that, pure tension at opposite ends of the taut line. After a full, round minute, I pull up a little to test the fish, to see if he's still there, and, man, he takes off, stripping line.

Mike has managed to tire his own fish, has it in close to the jetty, in amid the undulating seaweed. He holds his rod up high with one hand, holds the net in the water, slowly draws the tired beast toward him. How often we've lost fish at this stage! But with a clean swoop Mike nets it. Dinner! Mike, Mike! He brings it up on the jetty, puts his foot brazenly behind the fish's head, pushes the lure more brazenly with his naked fingers to release the hook. "Eight pounds?" he says, into the wind.

I take a quick look, nod—eight pounds, yep. I say, "Dinner," putting pressure on my own fish, gaining line slowly. The wind's loud, the water louder; the gulls are making a racket. Mike throws his hands in the air, comically victorious. Neither of us has caught a good fish in three weeks and two days. He kicks and nudges his catch with a kind of triumphant respect (blue sneakers) into a big flotsam-filled space between the jetty boulders where it can't flop back into the water, our own little fish vault. In five minutes it will be dead, no small matter.

Mike throws another cast. His Hopkins sails off into the sky, trailing glistening line under the darkening clouds. "Into the vortex!" he hollers. As always, I surge with pleasure unto laughter at the way he uses words, and the surge quadruples with the great thrash of fish feeding. It *is* a vortex, a living vortex, greedy and violent. The wind itself seems full of fish. My hair whips around my head, my pants flap. My feet are cold, but that's for later. Mike's twelve-foot fishing rod bends double, a blade of grass. The stranger's got a fish, too. His jacket whips in the wind. My fish is at the jetty now. I climb down the rocks, lean over the weed and surging foam, soaked now to the knees, keep tension on the line, grip the rocks with my toes. Seeing that the blue is well hooked I don't call for the net, but simply grab the heavy leader—don't slip, don't miss, don't fall in, *don't lose that fish*—grab it high so as not to get too close to those brutal, clenched jaws. And I scrabble back up, holding taut the whole strained relationship of fish and line and hand and self, grinning in the wind, make the jetty top, loft the fish, get the stranger's grin, get Mike's, lay the fish on the rock, bare foot on his side, lean to reach my pliers, work the hook out gently as I can, feel him all flex and muscle and ready to have my toes, scoot him quick into our vault between the jetty rocks, stand there looking in for just a moment, damn thankful, dinner, all right, an offering: Mike's fish, mine, ours. The fish are twins, over two feet long, sleek, the flash of sunlight from the struggling scales more the eponymous blue than the fish. They gasp. Dead they will only be grey. Alive, oh, alive they are blue and vicious, they roll their eyes, they stare, ready to twist and pounce and tear off your fingers, ready to tear off your nose and swallow it down, ready to flop with uncanny accuracy if you get too close, ready to get hold and make you pay for your cocky stance inside the last link of a food chain they well know to be cruel.

The frenzy doesn't stop, Mike's vortex, the press, the rage and leap, the roiling madness, the widening gyre. Baitfish try to fly, try to leave the ocean entirely, whole schools in the gap between waves, shining arcs cut through by bluefish, bluefish raging. Our lures swim through the boiling cauldrons, send the baitfish leaping in fear, attract the big boys, chomp and pull. After a half hour we've caught five fish each, two at eight pounds, five more at five pounds, one, Mike's latest, eleven pounds at least, the biggest I've seen. The varying weights are evidence of three schools feeding at once, thousands of individuals swimming at rocket speed after nourishment, converging on the rich Menemsha Harbor inlet.

And we are not the only lucky ones. On the other jetty, across that narrow inlet, twenty or thirty fishermen cast frantically. Mike and I have made and always make the long drive around Menemsha pond to Lobsterville expressly to avoid that crowd, and a good thing. A circus over there. Crossed lines, snags, lures in people's hair, sunset watchers in the way, little boys screaming, bluefish flopping onto the rocks then back into the water: mayhem, irritation, disaster mocking success. But the wind will blow them all away, it will, the wind likes empty rocks and winter.

"Incredible," our new chum says. He's maybe ten years older than I (as I am ten years older than Mike), more well dressed, strangely apologetic, as if he thinks we are Islanders and expects our contempt. He says, "I've never been in the middle of it like this! Only read about it! It's a convocation of schools! Could last for bloody hours!" His sweatshirt says IBM. He's lean, not a guy who drinks much beer.

Two men around Mike's age join us on the jetty, racing excited along the rocks, pulling the packaging off their brand-new rods. "Our first day," one of them says. "What do we do?" Mike gives them leaders from my box (Mike always unfailingly generous with my tackle), ties knots for them rather than spend the time to teach the difficult stuff. Before long and despite bad casts and dime-store bass lures, they're catching fish with the rest of us and shouting with triumph. I help them land their first fish. IBM helps them untangle their reels when the time comes. When there's plenty, one gives.

More seagulls arrive by the moment and feed noisily, snapping up tattered pieces of herring and mackerel and sand eel left by the blues, not lingering, knowing better than to sit on the water dangling feet in the midst of all those snapping jaws. More fishermen, refugees from the jetty on the Menemsha side, arrive running, frantically preparing their tackle. Now Mike and IBM and I are at the very head of the jetty together, prime position. I cast, hook a fish, lose him, reel a few feet, hook another, lose him, reel further, hook yet another not ten feet from the rocks, bring him in.

Next cast I hook a fish that shakes the lure free easily then bites it *again*, is caught. On several casts, two fish chase the lure, leaping, feinting, ten feet, twenty, till one prevails—strike! On one long cast, I think I've caught a sea monster. It pulls sluggishly to one side, then to the next, nothing like a bluefish. The line's so heavy it takes me twenty minutes to get the mystery catch to the jetty, where I see the problem: two big blues have struck at once. Bobby Robertini will be sorry he decided not to come!

"Pertinacious!" Mike shouts, and I laugh and laugh and laugh, cast again. What does he mean? Everything, everything! We are here, of substance!

Two hours pass. The feed is still wallopingly, splashingly, on. The blues race into the channel, feed in the harbor. They come up within a few feet of the jetty, where we can see their mouths open and slam shut, see the macerated pieces of green mackerel and flashing herring and wriggling sand eel, smell the sweet oil of the baitfish-slick the blues leave behind. The blues! They slap their tails, they splash, they leap. The water writhes unceasing with insane predation and wind and wave. The sun hits the horizon; the sky goes gradually orange, goes more quickly red, all those grand clouds to catch the light. The tourists applaud the sunset like passengers applaud a plane landed well though the pilot can't hear, like movie viewers applaud the screen, the director far away, far away, far away. They stare awhile in hopes of seeing the storied green flash. They get going home. We should too.

At ten blues apiece Mike and I pause to confer. He thinks we have enough to feed the entire Labor Day picnic a good chunk of fish. We have comically, fake pompously, promised to provide a bluefish dinner for each of the forty or so people who will by now have gathered at the Robertinis' house in Oak Bluffs. The joke was that we've caught nothing for the two weeks since the Robertinis have arrived, for longer than that, too, and the Robertinis have pretended, joshing, not to believe we have ever caught a fish at all, those fellows with their boat. The joke is we haven't been able to provide fish for *anybody*, much less the forty!

The sky goes black and starry behind us, deep violet ahead. The big clouds have hurried inland, dissipated over Boston. Hercules emerges above us, and Lyra, and Boötes, and the Big Dipper, and Venus is up, and reddish warring Mars. The frenzy, ungodly, goes on. We throw each catch back, careful not to wound those hard mouths. The jetty's getting very crowded. The tide has turned, is falling. The feed can't last. Across the channel the other jetty is a nightclub without bouncers, a dance floor with fishing rods.

We quit. Mike and I pack up and quit. Two guys move up the jetty to claim our spot. And now there is the problem of transporting twenty slippery fish. We think to fillet them on the beach, but at the picnic forty fillets won't make the impression twenty whole fish will make. I find a piece of lobster-trap rope the sea has disgorged, and we thread it in through twenty slackened mouths and out through twenty useless gills, carry the string between us, 150 pounds of fish, heavy. On the beach we settle in amongst the querulous gulls to clean fish, scaling them fast as we can—the party awaits—slicing each from anal vent to throat and pulling out swim bladders, hearts, livers, stomachs, intestines. In the very full stomachs we find sand eels, mackerel and herring, some whole, some bitten in half, packed in, stuffed in, no possible room for more—yet around the jetty the frenzy continues.

Mike and I, we throw the fish innards to the birds, who fight to taste them first. We grin and grin, can't stop, can't stop shaking our heads. We don't have to say a word. We love these fish. And it's finally happened: a perfect day's catch. We look at each other and cut bellies and laugh and look at each other and grin, thinking of the picnic to come. We look at each other and punch the other's arm and slap high fives and grin. We only feel bad for the young men down the jetty. It is their first day fishing, ever, and it will never be like this again.

Mike and I, we're late for the party, which only adds to the drama. What a cheer as we pull the string of gutted blues from the back of my truck! We're providers, triumphant! The emotions called forth are ancient! The males look maybe a little jealous, especially those guys in our band. My girl Juliet comes out of the house, glass of wine in hand, to see. She's proud in a way that has nothing to do with winning a game, with sports. She puts her arm around me, claiming me. Mike and I take hugs, get kisses, hug each other for a photograph with fish. Everyone crowds to see them, twenty big goddamned fish. Bobby Robertini curses, wishes cheerfully pissed that he'd been with us and not out on the boat with his frigging brothers: one flounder, lost. Dad Robertini comes out ceremoniously with five sharp knives, and five of us squat down to make fillets. The smell is clean, of nature, glorious. Later, Mike and I will toss the heads and spines and tails and fins back to the sea: food for lobsters, food for crabs.

Later still, he and I will fall out of touch.

A drunken Robertini uncle melts diced onions in lots of butter and Jack Daniel's; a cousin builds up the fire. Soon enough Mike and I are cooking fish, and soon enough again we all of us—everyone at that party—we all sit on the porch steps and on the bench by the volleyball net and in the warm kitchen and eat bluefish. That Jack Daniel's sauce is astonishingly good. There is nothing like bluefish one hour out of the sea.

Mike and I, we're beaming.

Duck Day Afternoon

In Maine every morning Juliet and I take the boys for a walk, what we call the circuit, down through the woods to the Temple Stream, and often through the stream in bare feet to Charlie's pasture, shoes back on, then up the hemlock hill and cross the stream again, hike back around on the tractor road through wildflowers in June, a grand loop, every day. We have a loop in Ohio, too, but that's different, a city loop through the park, along the avenue, down a back alley full of dogs behind fences, back to our street and home, the boys on leashes, tugging at our arms.

But in Maine Desi and Wally leap through the tall grasses like savanna animals, or even stop and graze like cows, in fact look like little cows, black and white both of them, Border collie crosses, our little herd of Holsteins.

One hot August morning Juliet and the doggies and I varied it a little and instead of crossing to the far pasture walked *in* the Temple Stream, old sneakers splashing in the current, the two of us people wading along maybe knee deep—oops, crotch deep, bellybutton! Shit! Cold!—on the sandy or rocky bottom in clear bright water with the dogs splashing or swimming strongly ahead or leaping up the steep banks into the revolution-era pasture our neighbor has put into conservation.

So I'm wet up to the chest, the dogs are soaked, Juliet's laughing at me, but stumbles in the middle of her pretty, pretty, inward laugh and falls in herself. And up and splashing at me and we're dissolved in laughter (seventeen years together!) and the dogs come to see and prance on the sandbar in an ecstasy of being with their people.

Wally trots off and Juliet and I aren't watching what he's doing, but wringing our shirts, glad it's hot as hell today. Suddenly, a duck comes flailing at us, just off the water, and here comes Wally following at a gallop, then Desi after Wally. Juliet yells and of course Desi-the-Well-Trained stops, but Wally, trained entirely by Desi (he's a dog's dog, that one), keeps going, and the duck seems injured, and immediately I think, well, Wally has hurt this bird. A female . . . mallard?

I scrabble up the deep intervale bank—it's seven feet high right there—and into the pasture, expecting to see carnage, feathers flying, but what I see is the pasture. Wally is out of sight in the tall grasses. Faraway, a good, long Wally-sprint away, hundreds and hundreds of yards, I see the duck flying beautifully up out of the little patch of trees that surround a cow watering hole there. Then I know what's happened—but didn't know ducks did it—the female was faking injury to draw the dog off her nest. This is confirmed when she flies back into the stream cut where Juliet and Desi still stand, flies in low, lands on the water noisily. I slide back down the bank, just as noisily. The duck flies at *Juliet,* low, flies past her, wings braked hard. Well, that's it for Desi. He's off like an Olympic swimmer exploding from the blocks, off and around the bend, out of sight behind the slow-flying duck.

So now both of the fellows are long gone, one decoyed to the middle of the old pasture, the other straight downstream, both hundreds of yards away from the duck nest implied by all this.

Juliet and I continue our walk, soaked, wading upstream. "Decoy!" I pant. "She decoyed the dogs!"

"The dogs are dumb," Juliet says. Of course she doesn't mean this. Our dogs are fission scientists, and Juliet knows it. She means *I'm* dumb.

I hiss, "The nest must be in here!" Dumb as hell.

As we come abreast of the spot from which Wally drew the duck out of the alders, mama duck comes back, low on the water, buzzes us from behind, rises up over our heads, flops down on the water in front of us, begins to thrash.

"She's hurt!" Juliet cries.

But the duck is not hurt. She crashes her way upstream, flailing one wing piteously, speed slower than for the dogs, adjusted for bipeds. But Juliet and I just stand there. We're ruining the duck's ancient strategy, not chasing her, just standing still too near her nest (or, as an autumn inspection will reveal, too near the entrance to the *path* to her nest, which turns out to be about *two hundred feet* into the pasture up there).

Wally has heard the commotion, and he's back, takes the bait. The duck adjusts her speed, rounds the upstream bend and is out of sight, Wally momentarily behind. But then Wally has a brainstorm, wheels in the water and splashes back to the overgrown bank where the nest must be. I call him off a low opening in the raggedy thicket of drooping streamside alders, where he snuffles, excited as I am, and begins to push his way in. But finally he heeds (I have to *growl* at him to achieve this) and he splashes disconsolately toward us.

Behind him, the male of the duck pair emerges from the alders, silently, and swims at us, beak agape, now quacking mockingly. It's not a mallard at all. It's that size but very plain and dark and I don't know what to make of him. Later I'll get a look in the many bird books around the house, and not be sure, later still describe it to my bird friend Bob Kimber who says "Black duck" right away and is right.

The male turns sharply downstream, turns his left wing out, and more or less walks on the water, dragging that perfectly healthy wing, gracefully pulling Wally downstream and off the nest. Desi's back, now, too, and our two proud pack members race downstream sticking to the sandbars till they are forced to swim. The duck eases into braked flight just above their heads, disappears around the downstream bend. The frantic dogs follow, and out of sight.

Juliet and I take the tractor ford and leave the stream, continue on the circuit, more or less *trot* away from the site of the hidden nest, knowing the dogs will race to catch up with us and forget the ducklings that must be in there (in the coming weeks without the dogs I'll get to count: nine ducklings, then eight, then seven, week by week, holding then at seven till they're big enough to fly).

I look to the sky and there are the two adult ducks, reunited, flying tandem in a tight, low circle overhead. They swoop in, finally, and land where we dogs and people had been standing, paddle in circles silently checking their success, then duck into the alders. The stream flows on, flows as if nothing had ever happened between ducks and dogs.

And here they come, Desi first, Wally behind, full speed over the sandbars, leaping and splashing, ears flying, galloping right past the hidden ducks, heedless, not even looking that direction: our boys! They always maraud in the direction we're headed. We do our best to protect the wild from what's wild in them, usually leave them home. But the wild has its own wiles, it does, and the duck his day.

Birthday

My dad calls a couple times, but I'm out walking. He leaves messages (Well, happy birthday. Your mom and I wanted to catch you and we'll keep trying), and I love him even more for this and Mom too—they're so dependable, like no one else in my life ever—100% dependable even at seventy-four years old, when they've got every excuse to forget. A birthday card has already come, a check inside it for a thousand dollars, a very lot of money still for Juliet and me, money which will go in the fund to buy a little more land, maybe, something permanent. And Pop has sent a tongue-in-cheek commercial e-mail card as well: my animated horoscope. It's going to be a good year! So say the stars, and this goodness and hope is the message from Mom and Dad: A good year! You're all right! Dad when he finally gets me on the phone next day says, "Well, what'd you do on your birthday?" And I say what he wants—twenty-two words: "Oh, you know, took a walk, went into town, had some friends over, one you've met, Barbara, re-member? Had a *nice* time." And he says yet another of the many great truths he has uttered in life, "Well, you're forty-six."

Mom wants to hear about my garden, which I got planted late this year. The garden, I tell her, is catching up.

Woke a bit groggy after strange dreams. One fragment is my standing in a country road and a car comes around the corner about to hit me. Flailing my arms in self-defense, I wake up pushing and flailing at Juliet. Who cries out, Hey!

She is not a car. All is well. She gets up to pee.

And then I lie there—3:30—sorting through the things of my mind (this is the watching time, as a scientist friend has told me it's called in some Asian cultures, and being up an hour or two at night a perfectly good thing if you don't call it insomnia and get panicked). What I seem to be thinking about are my careers both literary and university, such as they are, and various corners of what can only be called guilt. Juliet gets back to sleep quickly, her arm flopped over me. I'm thinking I should figure out how to leave The Ohio State University, leave Ohio, get back home to Maine all year. Couple more years. Pay my dues. Then come home.

Next dream (unknown woman and I watch in horror as our dogs fall four stories because of a missing fire escape) is later in the morning, and the day has dawned, mutedly bright. I was born at 6:45 A.M. on August 18, 1953, so am now, August 18, 1999, officially forty-six years old. There is no going back, except to sleep.

Wake again, and it is full morning and fully my birthday. How I used to love my birthdays! Only a very few years ago did this ticking of years become complicated for me at all. Still, I recall and nearly feel the old birthday glow. This is my day! I'm a Leo and it's my month. I love summer and it is summer, the season of my birth. I love Maine and we are in Maine.

Juliet remembers my pushing her in the night—finds this amusing now but with an edge of irritation. Beatles song goes through my head in paraphrasis: *They say it's my* birth-*day*. We make love in our ingrained way but sideways across the bed for a change, already thinking about what's coming, which is that we're going to try to get pregnant in the fall. Detested condom, however, this morning. Except for that, all very comfortable, very conjugal. Diagonal across the bed turns out pretty good because the dip in our old mattress bends us funny ways that challenge what's granted.

I'm forty-six. *Nah na na na nah-nah!* For the first time I think how close to fifty that is. Jesus. Four years more and I'm *fifty.* And yet the past four years—think of all that's happened, all I've done and not done. How fast those four each came and went, and how slowly. Very slowly. How long four years will be, how very long it will actually be until I'm fifty—a whole, entire high school career. A whole college career. Four years. The whole enormous gap of time between my big brother's age and mine when we were little (a gap of but vestigial significance now). And think how long it took the presidents to change: four-year terms, some doubled, some aborted. My presidents so far: Eisenhower, Kennedy, Johnson, Nixon, Ford, Carter, Reagan, Bush, Clinton. *Happy Birthday to* me, *yeah!*

✍

Regular breakfast, though for many years on my own I continued my father's tradition of something special—French toast, pancakes, that sort of thing. Today, I eat my regular breakfast, one thick piece of toast (this from a nice loaf of oatmeal-molasses bread from Nezinscot Farm's booth at the Friday farmer's market set up in the Park 'n' Ride lot in town), one banana, one pint of water. Then I do a chore or two. Sweep up the porch. Fill up my various birdfeeders, suddenly remembering my own present to myself, arrived by FedEx yesterday but as yet unopened: a new tube birdfeeder from L.L. Bean. I leave it in the box for the time being—it needs to be borne ceremoniously to a place foreordained, and I haven't figured the spot yet, just that it should be somewhere I can see it from my study window.

Juliet has sneaked downstairs at some point in the morning or night and put up the cheerful HAPPY BIRTHDAY BILL banner she made a few summers back. She'll have to go off to town to get some presents—that's more or less how we do things in this little duet of ours: last minute.

First bird of the day is a raven yelling in Dennis's box-elder trees next door—that's the land we're hoping to buy, five acres to add to our six, including Dennis's old barn, built 1820, but sagging and ready to fall. Dennis has moved his operation up the hill to a beautiful spread on high, the crest of Porter Hill. Second bird is a blue jay, also yelling. Nothing subtle this morning.

Juliet and the dogs go on around the woods loop so that I can wade the Temple Stream without Wally and Desi, who will only disturb whatever birds I might spot and splash away all thoughts. The idea, after all, here on my birthday, is to think. Off in the woods I can hear Jules yelling at Wally—he's chasing some animal or other.

I slip down the old mud beaver ramp and step straight into the stream the way the dogs like to do and just keep going, wading slowly, looking into the water, remembering the things I've found here on birthdays past, thinking maybe I'd find something today, too, a pretty safe prediction, because I find something or other in the stream daily, potsherds from nineteenth-century dumps, stream glass. But on my birthday those couple of years back I wanted to find something special for being suddenly over forty, and so I looked hard and suddenly saw a blue-green stone, not a gem, perhaps only a chunk of old pot, but very unusual and very lovely and bright, meaningful in my hand, and, since I'd been looking for it, maybe magical. In possible proof of the magic I accidentally dropped this wee stone (size of a raisin—I have it right here in my writing basket of totems for luck and wisdom, which are all the more powerful for my not really believing in them: scale from some huge fish, French car-wash token, tiny clam shell, tiny dried starfish, chunk of fool's gold, tiny pinecones, shapely driftwood chip from Quansoo beach in West Tisbury, mysterious Indian artifact from the Frying Pan River in Colorado, gas-station shirt-patch "Bill," polished picture jasper, two pieces soapstone, Mexican arrowhead, skeleton key, and as many more odds and ends), dropped it five times, six, and kept finding it even underwater and in the tousled and layered hay of Dennis's pasture, and finally, back home, and despite huge caution, dropped it on the porch and watched it roll and then fall between floorboards, so had to go underneath in the spider-webbed crawl space, where on my belly I recovered the thing and rushed it upstairs to my little basket, dropping it twice more on the stairs, then missing the basket from inches away—a lively stone.

Then there was last year, my walking along very self-consciously in the stream on my birthday, thinking I shouldn't think too hard about finding a surprise even as I was looking for my surprise, and suddenly there it was: a glowing marble in the stream, an old, old marble of blue and white with patches of brickish red, looking like the earth—tiny. Again, magical, mysterious, even though I don't believe in such things. What I do believe in, I would say, is *coincidence*. And in keeping a record of coincidence by filling a joss basket on my desk. And I believe in what's in the basket, all that stuff together by no coincidence (I rearrange it every time we move back and forth from Maine to Ohio): I believe at the very least that the basket is really there, the things in it really put there by myself.

I kept my fist on that marble like the earth, never dropped it, and now it's in my little basket of lucky things, top of the pile where I see it every day.

So I'm wading along on my forty-sixth birthday and not forty-six sloshing steps (I said *not* forty-six), not forty-six stream steps from the beaver ramp, there is an *eel*. A large, long, green, lovely *eel*, not long dead, maybe minutes dead. I've never seen an eel anywhere around here before, never caught one in fresh water, only seen some in brackish water, these swimming in on the estuary tide on beaches in Cape Cod and Martha's Vineyard at different times. An *eel*, like a cosmic joke (I mean, come on!), when I'm looking for something special for my birthday in the stream. This eel is not something to keep, unfortunately—won't fit in my fortune basket. I kick it up on the sandbar and just look at it. No marks to say why dead. Just dead. Barely. I pick it up and it twitches a little, the way fish do newly dead. An *eel*. Maybe someone had it for bait and tossed it in the stream? But this isn't a bait eel. And you don't use eels for bait up here. Maybe I just don't know about eels in rivers?

Have to look it up. So I bring it with me, for positive ID. It balances perfectly just at its vent, is very, very slippery, though as it dries out the slime gets tacky and holding on easy. I'm carrying an *eel*.

It's my birthday.

And on the gravel bar under the fallen hawthorne I find a small root system, not as big as my hand, bleached and polished, a sweet little sculpture, a keeper. But not a surprise—driftwood is the stream's constant product. So, I keep looking in the water. It's been raining a lot, and new shards will have turned up, and of course I'm not looking for any birthday surprises because looking for them isn't going to help find them. Hum-de-hum, just looking for the usual potsherds. I find some nice ones, then . . . a strange one. A curving odd piece of something or other, something certainly small enough for a luck basket that's only about four inches wide and two deep. The thing is a plate as if tectonic, a decurved plate off a *pool ball*—though I don't realize all this at first, figure it out over a minute or so, with growing excitement, as if yet another coincidence on yet another birthday were of even slight importance.

It's a cracked gutta-percha hunk of a pool ball, which I know not only because of the extrapolated size of the sphere, but because the chunk I happen to have includes the *number*—my tiny tectonic plate is from an *eleven ball*. Knowing the eel wouldn't fit in my basket nor keep in any case, the stream has added *this*. Three years running, these surprises from the Temple Stream.

But walking back with it and my eel and also the hand-size driftwood root system (which lovely thing is now on the picnic table) and many potsherds I'm wondering and wondering about the significance of the number eleven, if any. At eleven, what was I up to on my birthday? Worrying about going into sixth grade, certainly. West School in New Canaan, Connecticut. Probably back a few weeks from Boy Scout camp. A lot of roaming in the woods those summer days, a certain amount of fishing. The year would have been '64, which if you reverse the numbers says forty-six, meaninglessly. But, Hey, Pop, was that one of the years you took me to a Yankees game? Or one you took me to Freedomland (an amusement park then, but later and now the site of the famous housing project called Co-op City)? My birthday cake at eleven would have been angel food cake with no icing, my favorite. Or with half no icing and half chocolate if Dougie and I were sharing that year he turned five.

Well, you can try too hard to find meaning in these things, seven come eleven.

⟋

I put down the goods in a pile including the eel in order to train binoculars on a midsize hawk flying and circling and trying to gain altitude and looking down inspecting the field for potsherds, no doubt. He's got a good fantail, long, not too close to his body. Primaries are translucent against the sky—lovely. *Hawks in Flight* says it's a Red Shouldered. I'm never too confident trying to identify hawks. But Red Shouldered seems to fit, given the size of the bird and his tail shape and wing "windows." He gives me a long, long look, spiraling up and westward and out of sight over the trees, reminding me that I saw a kestrel the other day at the top of the dying popple—a real individual, missing a tail feather, like a kid with a gap tooth. I pick up my mysterious eel and again it *twitches*.

I stop at the dying popple (poplar, or eastern aspen) to look under it for the kestrel feather. Not there. The kestrel could have lost that feather anywhere and when, but since it's my birthday and I've already got an eel and pool-ball shard, I think to look for it. Underneath the popple all the grass and jewelweed are freshly crushed and matted. Deer bed? Then there's my favorite sound, hummingbird, and I quickly find him in the jewelweed under the dying popple. I have seen hummers right here regularly this summer, but never when holding an eel.

And this reminds me that I rescued a hummingbird from the barn yesterday. She (was female) was buzzing up against the old storm-door window I'd put where the outhouse entrance used to be, just trying to solve the problem of an invisible barrier, unpanicked. My presence did panic her, though, and she got frantic, up and down, up and down on the big window. I tried a gentle hand grab, but she didn't like that, so I took a flowerpot and covered her and some of the spiderwebs too, and her head got caught up in the spiderwebs and she must surely have felt she was being eaten. Next, I tried to pull the pot back off the window, but her head was bent back by a strong strand of spiderweb. She made the most piteous sound— a faint bleating like a dog crying ever so softly. So, Jesus, I just acted decisively and pinched the web free and got her in the pot with my hand and rushed her outside and put the pot down and found her in there quite tangled in webs, but one wing free, neck bent back. Felt horrible if I hurt her! I pulled the webs off her, handling her gently, first off her face and beak so her neck could relax (it did) and then off her other wing, holding her as gently as I could, and she flew straight to the plum tree, no problem, and stopped there to finish the cleanup. I know hummingbirds use spiderwebs in their nests, so she must have known something about their sticky nature, and I can't be blamed for spiderwebs, though maybe for the mess of the barn.

Here it's time for a leak, so I drop my prizes, eel, ball shard, driftwood root, pull out with somewhat eel-sticky hand my own version of what John Updike has Rabbit Angstrom (in *Rabbit Is Rich*) call his "pink wreckage," my own poor eel, not wreckage yet, precisely, though it's got some miles on it. Forty-six years, it has, come to think of it, neatly cut, veteran of college in the seventies, and more STD's major and minor than it likes to talk about: gentle dumb beast, never a weapon, instrument of fatherhood to come, beloved corner of myself, same status in my personal body hierarchy as a knee, really, or a foot, or my nose (despite what some women seem to think), not so noble as its friends the hands, not so busy as the mouth. And I mark my place there in the field, sign for coyotes to sniff and raccoons to avoid (gardeners say), my own meaningless addition of moisture and acids and nitrogen to this spot where the millions also micturate.

And I head back up the hill to the house in Dennis's field, holding the eel in one hand, the eleven-ball shard, small root system in the other, no kestrel feather, chin up, marching proudly. Straight to Juliet's studio to show her my prizes. She's painting, but the eel is interesting enough, in my estimation, for me to interrupt her peace for show-and-tell. She's surprised and a little grossed out. I ask for her Polaroid camera and she shakes her head but it's my birthday so she can't make too much fun of me, and out on the deck I take a picture of my eel next to a tape measure pulled out. The fish is twenty-seven inches long. Upstairs I find my species books for fish—then remember the eleven-ball shard. Where is it? It's down on the picnic table. I rush downstairs and outside and retrieve the shard but stop helplessly in the kitchen and eat a couple handfuls of cereal, and only then back upstairs, where I look immediately in MacClane's fish book, and then Peterson's—these are both saltwater guides—and find "Freshwater Eels." "A single catadromous species *Anguilla rostrata*, or American Eel, is caught by sports fishermen in salt and brackish water," MacClane says.

Catadromous means lives in the sea, spawns in freshwater. Peterson says:

AMERICAN EEL—anguilla rostrata.
Identification: greenish brown, sometimes yellowish below. *Dorsal fin begins far back, above a point between pectoral fin and anus. Lower jaw longer than upper;* both jaws have well-defined lip folds. Rear nostril round, located in front of eye. Vertical (dorsal, anal, and caudal) fins continuous. Size: Females to 1.5 m (5 ft.) but rarely more than 90 cm (3 ft.); males decidedly smaller. Range: Fresh and coastal waters throughout eastern N. America, to northern S. America, including the Bahamas and other large islands. Remarks: Adults enter sea during winter and early spring. Habits at sea unknown.

Yes, yes, some habits are best left unknown. But you asked, Pop, you asked what I did on my birthday!

By now it was well past time to get writing (*happy birthday to me, yeah!*). So back upstairs and to work for a couple of hours. And there I am writing more or less contentedly on the subject of kingfishers, and then suddenly I'm like: Where's that eleven-ball shard? I rush downstairs and find the fragile-seeming thing in the kitchen, but it's safe and sound, maybe tougher than it looks (it had lived in someone's dump and then the

Temple Stream fifty or sixty or a hundred years, after all). And then I get the idea to make a cucumber salad for my birthday party. So to the garden, seven beautiful cukes, and quick since it's writing time peel them and slice them into our biggest (huge) bowl, and slice in three fat onions, and run back down to the garden in the hot sun for parsley, and back in the kitchen rinse that and chop it up quick-quick and into the bowl, and mix water and vinegar one to one, a pint each, and a cup of sugar and pour that over the cukes, make room in the fridge, and bang, I'm done.

Back upstairs and sit down to write, and I'm like: Where's that eleven-ball shard?! And back down and find it on the woodstove, and get it upstairs with force of will, focussing on it, and into the little basket on my desk.

I write a few sentences more on kingfishers, the way they flee upstream or downstream ahead of a canoe coming at them, startled each time they see you again when you catch up, three or four sentences, not quite getting it right. But I work those sentences, and work them a little more. Then go to visit with Juliet downstairs in her studio, where she's leaning over a large canvas (four feet by six feet) laid out on the floor, splashing heavily thinned oil paint on it, very bright pink. She's not bugged by my intrusion, but only because it's my birthday. "Do you think it's *fumy* in here?" she says. (We smile at the word *fumy* every time because that was my college girlfriend Susan's nickname for fartsome me.) Juliet's new box fan, which is the fifth one we've bought in recent years—where do they go?—is on a chair in front of one of the narrow Anderson windows some old owner of our house installed in this room. The better choice for a fan window is painted closed, one of the original sash windows (more than a hundred years old, glass bubbled and veined), and now I've got a project far from kingfishers and laptops. I search the shed and then the woodshop till I find my pry bar, and using it and knife and hammer and screwdriver and gentle persuasion I open that window while Juliet paints. The fan just fits—perfect.

Then back to work writing.

When I come up for air, Juliet has lunch ready. She's wrapped seven presents and these are on the table, and after the sandwiches (goat cheddar from Nezinscot with fresh cuke, fresh tomato, tough lettuce, all from the garden, lots of mustard, thick slice of Nezinscot bread, a carrot, and a little of the aforementioned cucumber salad—in summer we don't eat much meat). I open all of them—laughing with pleasure—some are gags, but there is a very nice shirt in there and a Leatherman tool inspired by the one a certain father of mine wears at his belt always: an ingenious folding knife, screwdrivers, file, scissors, bottle opener, and full-size pliers. Good stuff, which goes on my belt immediately in its leather case. Seventeen years Juliet and I have been an item, and she gets the presents right.

After lunch, I settle in for a nap in the hammock, which is hooked at one end to a big white pine, at the other to a bigger balsam fir—you lie there in the tent all those branches make and look out at the hills and sniff the breezes and the balsam. Desi and Wally lie underneath. This is peaceful, plenty warm, a lovely day. I read in a British book assigned me for review by Laurie Muchnick at *Newsday* down there in New York City. Laurie I like. The book, I'm not so sure.

Snore.

I wake up and read a little more (some unpleasant British woman's adventures in Australia), then stare a little out at the hills, then up and at 'em. Quick circuit through the woods with the boys, then upstairs for some e-mail, which is a mistake, lots of university vibes in there, lots of Ohio vibes, too many for a birthday in Maine. But birthday greetings from various friends, including Susan, the very college girlfriend who called me Fumy, now mother of two and a successful music professor. I bet her husband farts plenty.

So to town—Farmington, Maine, a very sweet place—to find the post office closed (it's after five already!), and the bookstore closed—and all the stores closed, actually, no savvy there about competing with national chains and strip malls. This nine-to-five stuff has got to go. I'll have to buy myself my birthday book tomorrow. Nina is open—gourmet shop. I say it's my birthday (*Nah na na na nah-nah!*) and she gives me a break on three bottles of wine for my party tonight. And I get a little *mousse truffée*, and some exotic crackers, and a good loaf of bread, and some *chèvre*, and a bag of candied ginger, and some other goodies. But I've forgotten any money, or my checkbook, so Nina puts it on a tab for me, knowing that a tab will get me back in the store, and that I'm a sucker for everything she's got in there.

As I'm leaving, her friend our housesitter slips in. I haven't seen him—not once—since June when we got back here. He says he's looking for a new place. Well, we'll see what happens with him this fall. I ask about the money he still owes on bills. He tells a long story about nailing his hand to a board with the pneumatic nail gun at work. And then hints at wanting to store his stuff at our house even if he doesn't come back. Not to worry. I smile and nod and stay noncommittal, and I'm pleased at my quiet reaction to him. Last couple of summers I've been less quiet with him. But he's all we've got! Nina tells him it's my birthday, and he gives me a hell of a warm handshake, and you know, I have to like him, too.

Quick stop for ice cream at Gifford's. These trips to town are important—I don't make them enough. In fact, haven't left the house for, like, six days! All that forest to roam in! Tomorrow maybe I'll hit the Friday farmer's market again, say hi to the handsome Nezinscot Farm woman (Juliet and I both have crushes on her—she's all earth and sun and muscles), and to Carla from Hoof 'n' Paw Farm, who is a psychotherapist and grows great vegetables.

And home, trusty red pickup, my 1984 F-150, just smooth thoughts in my head, not too fast (truck or thoughts), no cars behind me, through the big curves and onto our road, following the Temple Stream. It's getting near six and I've got to cook. Home I crack a birthday Guinness and drink a little of it and start pulling things out of the fridge. We'll have vegetables skewered on the grill, whatever fish Juliet brings home from Shop 'n' Save, little red potatoes from Hoof 'n' Paw. Cucumber salad is already made, thanks to my divagations during writing time, has already been sampled at lunch, found toothsome.

And we've got wine. And beer. And that bottle of champagne my younger brother, Douglas, gave us when he visited, if anyone wants champagne. I contemplate the guest list, which is all last-minute, and all women by happenstance (pal Wes is away, for example), something a little different this year, especially different from my fortieth, that fiery ascent from youth, when I had ten guys over—all guys—and we sat around a campfire out by the plum trees and drank whiskey and laughed a lot and I *puked* the next morning! One last crapulous puke for old time's sake! Trying to prove I wasn't old, is my guess. In fact, I was perversely *happy* to puke, proof as it was that I was still a fool and not some kind of older-and-wiser relic.

I listen quick to the answering machine: birthday messages from sister Janet, in-laws Frank and Ursula, oldest friend Kurt, champagne Dougie. Then outdoors to light the fire in our Wal-Mart grill, much rust and mayhem there, but it works well enough. Whole bag of charcoal. And rush back in to start cutting vegetables. Put on the radio: "All Things Considered." Sip of stout now and again. Pleasant radio voices. Dulcet breezes. Rose-breasted grosbeak out at the feeder. Now this is nice. The Way Life Should Be, as the sign says when you drive into Maine from away, and true.

Gorgeous Juliet comes bustling home from groceries, still covered in paint. Has she bought a cake? That is a secret! She's got good things for our party. More beer, for example. And she's got swordfish. *Endangered species!* Oh, my god. But, I don't say a peep—it's a beautiful fresh cut, and I love swordfish, haven't had any for years and years—but. But quiet, and add ocean fisheries to university and housesitter for things that came up on my birthday to worry silently about. Off Juliet goes with the dogs on a circuit through the woods.

This is the practical part of the day. I put the fish in a pan of white wine to marinate on some sort of vague theory I've got about swordfish getting dry on the grill (since affirmed by chef friend), then finish cutting up peppers, tomatoes, mushrooms, onions, zukes. Spear 'em on skewers. Brush with olive oil. Check the fire. Juliet's invited Jan and Barb, both a little older than I. And Jan's invited her daughter, who's just out of college and visiting. And Liza has invited a girlfriend.

I cook. I sip stout. (I *am* stout.) Juliet is back, all smiles. She gets in the shower.

Happy, happy birthday, baby!

I, I am forty-six.

First old Saab is Babsy, and the dogs go nuts barking. I let them out back as she comes in the front: old trick. She's looking great, fit and trim, tough old girl, face bright and wry, all of her sunburned from working in the garden and outside around the house she built entirely on her own. Her gruff man left her a couple years back, but she's over that, now, way over it, at that stage where being alone gets to be fine, all confidence and possibility. She's a painter. Every time I see her I think of one of her poignant and sometimes wacky self-portraits (a great one is herself in bed with a broken heart, phone at her side). Every face she makes is in one of them. Several portraits hang around our house. Several appear in my head now as she greets me and hugs me hello.

Then Jan's there—this is Maine, no "fashionably late" here—newer Saab. The dogs greet that carload. Jan just split up with her husband (also a friend—I try not to play favorites!) last year, come to think of it, and she's just past the rebound relationships and into the taking-stock phase, no fun, but she's doing pretty well. She's an artist, too, works with computers mostly now, incredible giant printouts of image and text. Her daughter, Liza, looks like her, and looks like Jim, too. Pretty, petulant face, thick dark Italian hair, slim hips, walks with a sashay, falling-off army pants, bellybutton showing. Her friend Cory is shorter, sturdier—very lovely, too, her eyes just coruscating with humor and intelligence and energy. And they are both unconsciously flirtatious in that way twenty-two-year-olds can be with old farts like me—feeling completely safe, they pump out all their charm, and completely safe, they keep it coming. Barb has a daughter their age, so she's quite comfortable with their youth. Jan, she's comfortable too. Juliet, too, and the kids love Juliet. We're all laughing away, very different kinds of people, very different knobs and quirks, fitted together snugly like jigsaw puzzle pieces for the evening. I've got the fire ready, the food prepped, and all is well on my birthday.

Juliet wants to do something in the kitchen—*birthday cake*, I don't let myself think—so I'm sent out. The younger women accompany me. Neither Cory nor Liza has been here to our house before. I walk down to the garden with them, the three of us holding beers, and they aren't awkward at all, but laughing with each other as I quiz them about school and plans for fall like a perfectly typical old fart of an English professor, which is exactly what I am. Liza already knows me, but Cory isn't sure how to comport herself. They've both got acts for being around friends-of-parents, secondary acts for profs, but I don't want to see those masks, give them what clues I can with body English and eyes: You two go ahead and say whatever you want, be yourselves.

The sunset is in progress, glorious deep orange under high clouds rising in perspective off of Mount Blue. I mean, really, *unusually* vivid color, and it lights up everything around us. The young women aren't ironic about this, but gaze out at all the big color and let it fill their faces. And the color just gets more intense after the sun falls through the last ridge of cloud and below Spruce Mountain, which is the shoulder of the more imposing Mount Blue. The fiery orange goes floral pinks then a heavy, living red.

"Fuck wow!" Liza says, coining a phrase I have used since.

Cory checks me for language opprobrium, finds none.

"Like tripping," I say, that old saw, trying to break the generational ice, but it's completely true for once—this is trippy as hell—the sky actually seems to be raising itself up over us, this ridge of cloud coming in heralding tomorrow's rain moving briskly and seemingly upward and over us, still fully lit, lighting us and everything around us, but moving, too, expanding, pushing out over us.

"A man after my heart!" Liza squeals, meaning about the tripping. Cory giggles at her old pal's openness and raises her hands to the sky and well, *fuck wow!* We all slug at our beers. These girls are *partiers*. They've let me know, and it's good to be trusted by anyone, but especially by these young women, these lovely, brainy young women, with all their plans and mistakes and loves and successes and endless days ahead of them.

Back at the house I bustle. Swordfish on the grill, vegetable skewers around it, close the lid for smoky flavor and carcinogens. Tablecloth on the deck table (a beautiful old cedar rig, owned by our housesitter, actually, so another friendly nod to him). And Barb and Jan set the table and open two bottles of wine while Juliet and the younger women talk seriously about art and then life—no cussing—art and life with their arms folded seriously in front of them, all nodding with the truth by the cold woodstove as the screen door bangs and the food bowls swing past. Juliet is someone other women like immediately, young or old.

I rush dinner to the table, and everyone helps, salads and potatoes and fish and vegetables, and we're all a little buzzed from beer as we dig in. The fish is unbelievably good, moist, fresh, sweet, tender. And the rice is nice. And the vegetable skewers are awesome! Cory says. Everyone buzzes in delight, even Liza, who is supposed to hate fish. And the salad is great and the wine is fine, and we toast (*We're gonna have a good time!*). Just a very nice meal on the deck (I built this deck with my dad and a college-kid helper in two weeks, three years back) with no bugs and with four candles and both beautiful young women across from me. And beautiful Juliet beside me—also funny as hell, my own wife—and lovely Jan to my left hand and handsome Barbie at the other end of the table. Barb telling us about a new boyfriend. Lots of general boyfriend talk and much laughter. And Cory says sadly that she and her boyfriend have just parted.

"Oh, I enjoy breaking up!" spouts Liza in response. She's abominable! We laugh, and laugh some more. Jan asks if I did anything special for my birthday.

I tell the eel story at boring length, I admit, but it's my birthday, tell the whole story of looking for surprises from the river, and finding them. It's risky material, in a way; I've never told anyone but Juliet about my lucky basket, for example. This is private stuff. But it's me and it's my birthday and I tell the story and that's the way it is. Cory and Liza watch me closely as I speak: odd man. Barbie looks at me skeptically: this kind of stuff, she never knew about me. Jan keeps her eyebrows raised in what might be interest. Juliet, she's weighing when to break in and change the subject, but it *is* my birthday. She lets me go on. And I tell them about the eleven-ball shard, trying for some irony, but now, for a moment their interest flairs: what could eleven refer to? What meaning there? What magic?

"Eleventh hour!" Liza says ominously.

"November," says Cory.

"Eleven lords aleaping," says Barbara, the cynic.

"Age of puberty?" says Jan.

"Football team," says Cory. This is funny, somehow, and we all laugh.

"I've got some new paintings," Juliet says.

And off we go on that subject, a good damn thing.

As the food disappears, I remember the bottle of champagne that's been in the fridge all summer, go get it, pop it open with a dramatic if amateurish splash on the table. The older women, they're red wine. But Liza's eyes light up, and Cory's, and within ten minutes they've drunk the entire bottle between them. And any reserve they may have shown at dinner, any deference to their elders, any uneasiness around Mom and mom-types, any queasiness about eels and the secret superstitions of middle-aged men, all that's gone.

Jan and Barb clear the table. Juliet has disappeared somewhere. Then they're all singing: Happy Birthday to You. And the lights go out and here comes Juliet bearing this nice store cake, angel food in half chocolate icing, half bare, and four candles burning, the whole familiar script, four candles instead of forty-six or forty-seven, which I blow out succinctly. No one will be spanking me. My secret wish is for love all around. Barb's got a story about the guy who built her studio. And Jan a story about her ancient father. I'm quiet, now, having told my stories. Juliet tells her funny story about being alone in Greece, with its awful ending: some Greek businessman squeezing her neck in an alley and her drunken escape.

Cory tells the funniest story I've maybe ever heard, about getting caught stealing from the Peanut Farm (which is a little gift shop in Farmington, owned by people we all know well). Then Liza: a riotous tale of breaking up with a loser boyfriend! We are screaming with laughter. Then Cory again, a story about getting caught in a fraternity riot at school in Arizona—she does the most perfectly hilarious imitation of herself holding a beer as everyone but she punched and rumbled and finally ditched when the cops came, and how nothing happened to her at all, though she never moved. The table's covered with plates and wineglasses and bowls and odd scraps of food (the dogs work the under-table buffet), and we're all sitting around it practically dancing, turning and twisting and throwing our hands in hilarious gesture, flinging our heads back in laughter. Laughter, laughter, and it echoes out into the empty woods.

But suddenly we hear tires screeching down the road, someone peeling out with unusual violence, peeling out over and over, backing up, peeling out, engine roaring, and then we hear a woman's voice yelling, *Go away!* Hoarse and afraid, that voice, and it keeps going on. *Get out!* I'm scared of the guy who lives down there, no doubt about that, no chance I'm going to stroll down there that quarter mile and have a word with him. Instead, I call the cops.

And pretty soon, over the repeatedly screeching tires and the continued yelling and screaming, we hear the super-tuned engine of a cop car coming over Porter Hill nine-hundred miles an hour, and see his headlights swing across the fields below us, and hear him stop down the road, hear his door slam. Then we hear this good officer talking. The miscreant must be someone he knows. Miscreant belligerent, officer soothing—we can just barely hear the tones, the too-human sound waves carrying over the dew-wet fields as they might over a lake, carrying in the clear air, still night. Then a loud *Fuck you!* And more screeching tires, sweep of headlights, roar of engine, changing gears, up and over Porter Hill. Then some sound of the woman berating the cop, too. What a job he's got! Shouting from the woman followed by his calm tones—much drama—until it all fades to quiet, nothing, and the night is around us.

We're all quiet then, too. Except for my saying that I'd never heard anything like this in seven years here. Of course the fireworks had to come tonight. Some nice neighborhood you'll think we've got here. And then the cop car, cruising slowly, back over Porter Hill.

We at the birthday party all sip wine, no eyes meeting. Whoa! The wild interlude (my neighbors on all sides having heard the same noises and having also called the police will talk with us about the eerie tire-screeching of that night for months), the dog-day disturbance, has stopped us cold. Then Cory again, bless her heart, breaks the spell with a tale of terror—apropos— from her college. Men and their fucking violence. This guy in her dorm. But Liza's got a funny example, and then Cory a funnier one yet, and before long we're all laughing again. *Fuck wow!* But really, the night is about over.

Eleven o'clock already. We get up one by one and clear the table, assemble finally in the kitchen amid lots of smiles and last Happy Birthdays and more stories and a couple more plates in the sink and dishwasher, plans for the coming weeks, a couple of preliminary goodbyes.

Cory says, "Hey, show us that eel!"

"Agh," says Liza.

It's in the refrigerator, plastic bag. I pull it out. Jan just doesn't want to see. Juliet has seen it already, so the two of them back away and talk their own talk, hug by the door, intermediate goodbyes.

"Ick," says Liza, as I open the bag.

"That's an eel, all right," says Barbie wryly. She has seen it all. "That's a hell of an eel."

And, I don't know, suddenly metaphor takes over, and it's like I'm showing them my *cock*. Liza, at least, recoils just the way she might if I did, has had enough, joins her mom and Juliet. Barbie drifts inward, lost in her own thoughts, turns back to the sink, stacks a plate or two, gives a yawn. Cory's interested in a clinical kind of way, the nurse of our metaphor. She says, "Show me the head." And I do, and it's just an eel, that's all, a fish of the sea swum all the way to our place for my birthday, habits at sea unknown.

Goodbye, goodbye. Off go the Saabs into the night. Juliet and I do some more straightening and cleaning. Midnight, and we're in bed, the warmth of the day still suffusing our upstairs room, a nice breeze sneaking through the screens to cool us. By dawn it'll be cold, but we're snug.

And then there's the roar of an engine, and more of that goddamned ghostly screeching, three or four passes by our drunken neighbor in front of his house, then one good one in front of our house, then nothing, just silence.

"You have a crush on Cory," Juliet says kindly.

"Who wouldn't?" says I, knowing Juliet has one, too, and all the world, a crush on the young.

"That is true," says Jules.

We lie there in the dark, and the day is done, and I am forty-six, Pop, thanks to you and Mom and every lucky chance these 16,801 days, and one more day down.

Scioto Blues

If you move to Columbus, Ohio, from Farmington, Maine, you will not be impressed by the landscape. It's flat around Columbus and the pre-prairie rivers move sluggish and brown. In Maine you pick out the height of flood on, say, the Sandy River, by the damage to tree trunks and the spookily exact plane made by ice and roaring current tearing off the lowest branches of riverside trees. In Columbus you pick out the height of flood on the Olentangy or Scioto rivers by the consistent plane attained by ten thousand pieces of garbage, mostly plastic bags, caught in tree branches.

Always in the months after I moved I was looking for a place to run the dogs, Wally and Desmond, who are Maine country dogs used to the unlimited woods. We started on a subsidiary athletic field at Ohio State—long, kick-out-the-jams gallops across mowed acres, lots of barking and rumbling—then leashes to cross Olentangy Boulevard and a parking lot, so to the Olentangy River (my students call it the Old and Tangy), where the boys swam hard just across from the Ohio Stadium, known as The Shoe, in which the football Buckeyes famously play.

By the time the university started building the gargantuan new basketball arena in the middle of our running field, the dogs and I had found Whetstone Park, a big urban preserve a couple of miles upstream, just across the river from Route 315, which at that point is six-lane, limited-access highway. Really, Whetstone's a lovely place, well kept, used in multiple ways, though not much in winter, always the sounds of 315 in the air like a mystical waterfall with diesel power and gear changes. There are athletic fields, a goldfish pond, picnic areas, tennis courts, basketball courts, an enormous and important rose collection in a special area called Park of the Roses, just one section (about three miles) of an all-city bike path, tetherball, speed bumps, a library branch (in satisfying possession of my books), fishing spots on the Olentangy River.

Which runs through Whetstone after a scary trip through a couple of suburban towns (Route 315 its constant companion), through a dozen new developments and several parks, past or near at least six shopping malls, also through the backyards of people who love the river, love it to death. Indeed, the detritus at its banks in Whetstone is emphatically suburban. Plastic grocery and other store bags of course dominate, festooning the trees in various colors, the worst of which is the sort of pinky brown that some stores use in a pathetic and surely cynical attempt to imitate the good old kraft paper of the now fading question, "Paper or plastic?" The best colors are red and blue, because at least there's that moment of thinking you see a rare bird. Garbage bags are part of the mix, too, but heavier, so lower in the trees.

Certainly plastic soft-drink bottles come next in sheer numbers. These things float best when someone upriver has put the cap back on before flinging, perhaps out of a car window. Or perhaps not flung, but only left beside a car in a parking lot along with a neat pile of cigarette butts from the emptied car ashtray. Come to think of it, these bottles are probably seldom thrown directly into the river. The plastic walls are thin, so plastic bottles aren't always the long-distance travelers you'd think. Cracks let water in, and silt. The bottles don't end up often in trees, either, because they are light enough and smooth enough for the wind to knock them free. They are everywhere, though. They rule.

Tires occupy their own category, and come in two sorts: with and without wheels. Those with wheels are heavy but float, so end up high on logjams and in trees; those without wheels get caught up in the silt and mud and form strange ring-shaped silt islands or, buried deeper, show just a little tread as part of a sandbar, or deeper yet, disappear from the world of light and air entirely, perhaps to emerge in a century or two, or a millennium, or more. They aren't going anyplace.

Next there are car parts other than tires. Like bumpers and doors and hoods. These must be dumped at riverbanks, is my guess, off the edges of parking lots built too close to the water, then carried by floods. Occasionally, too, a whole car gets in the water, and slowly demonstrates the second law of thermodynamics: all things seek randomness. Entropy continues its work of unworking, and the car spreads downstream. The iron involved is at least no problem.

Aerosol containers make a strong showing in the river, those former dispensers of paint and freon and deodorant and foot spray and whipped cream and so forth. Indestructibly happy bobbers, these canisters are capable of long trips, clear to the Gulf of Mexico, I'm sure, and before long into the oxygen-free, Lake Erie–size dead zone the Gulf now boasts. But some do get up high in tree crotches and last there for years—decades if they're of stainless steel. WD-40 as a product gets a special mention here, for the paint on the outside and the oil film on the inside keep these cans alive and recognizable for years wherever they roam.

Newspaper and other print matter turns up but disappears just as fast, leaching what it leaches into the water. A special category of printed matter I ought to mention is pornography, which I often find high and dry, the park being its entry point into the river. *Juggs* was one magazine I happened across. It had many photos in it of women who'd had obviously harrowing operations. Also, some kind of trading cards that featured various young women naked. These I discovered clipped neatly by the bark flaps of a shaggy hickory at the eye level of a large adolescent or small man, footprints and dribbles beneath, the whole gallery abandoned after our riparian onanist had done his work.

Other items: prescription medicine bottles, but not in abundance; mattresses common, usually appearing as skeleton only, that is, the springs; pens of endless varieties, mostly ballpoint, ubiquitous, some working; twisted shopping carts; tampon tubes of pink plastic made by, I believe, Playtex (plenty of these, from flushes, giving lie to the idea that sewage is well managed upstream); guardrails; lengths of rope of various types; lengths of cable, mostly Romex; joint-compound buckets (but these are fast fillers and sinkers and join the silt banks permanently with their tire friends and with broken glass bottles).

Glass. Any glass that turns up (except tempered, as in windshields) at least turns back to sand, squandering its legacy of power and fire. The rare complete glass bottle with lid does float by, but these are goners, baby; first rock they encounter and it's *smash*, step one toward beach glass for kids to find. Eyeglasses you'd think would be rare, but just in the last year I've found three pair, lenses intact.

Planks. Now, planks hardly count, being trees, but often planks have nails, which hardly count, either, come to think of it, being iron. Then again, planks are often painted, so they do add to the color stream—what's that purple? What's that turquoise? A bright yellow board I saw once caught up in a willow was particularly startling.

Now, pieces of Styrofoam are important in this trash system. There are blue pieces often enough, occasionally green, but white is most common. Everywhere are the tiny cells that make up the product—billions of bright spheres, with samples worked into every handful of mud. Packing popcorn, too, everywhere. Cups, sure, but these don't last long. Coolers predominate. Then chunks, which must come from packing materials. Then even bigger chunks, unexplained on the Olentangy, and nowhere as big as the huge chunks found on beaches on the seacoast in Maine, parts of boats or floats or who knows what. And oh, yes, speaking of beach flotsam, boat parts are common too, even on rivers, and even in the Olentangy. Fiberglass boards, not too big, or rowboat seats, or canoe prows, rarely. This is not a sport river.

Though there are fishermen, and there are fish. Catfish and smallmouth bass, most notably. And the fishermen leave their own class of trash: broken fishing rods; lots of line tangled in branches above; bobbers hanging from power lines; lead weights. Lead is poisonous, of course, so a special mention. Also lures sometimes, hanging as well. Or just plain hooks in a branch, dried up worms. Little boys, mostly, though lots of retired men like to fish the river. Also men who don't look old enough to retire, maybe some of those guys who have I'D RATHER BE FISHING bumper stickers on their bumpers (and their bumpers still attached to their cars).

The fisherfolk also leave packaging for hooks and snells and bait and so forth. American Eagle is one of the brand names you see frequently in the mud. And plastic bait cups are just everywhere, their lids not far behind, these packed by local concerns, sometimes with an address printed along with the logo so that I can mail the shit back to them (yes, I'm a crank). They may not be responsible for their customers, but they should care where their names turn up.

Some of the other garbage comes with brand names, too: Budweiser, Wendy's, Kmart, Big Bear, Dow Chemical, General Electric, Goodyear, to name just a few. All these big names sticking up out of the mud! It's like some apocalyptic ad campaign!

Now for the less tangible. Apart from the major chunks in the Old and Tangy River, there is the smell, and the smell must come from somewhere. It's not horrible or anything, not even pervasive, but when the dogs get out of the river there's not only the usual river smell—mud and oxygen and hydrogen and fish and pungent organic rot—there's something else, one notch below healthy on the dial. My amateur analysis is as follows: equal parts motor oils, fertilizers, and straight human shit. Also shampoo and detergent, the faintest sickening edge of perfume.

Which leads me to the foam, good bubbly stuff that can stack up to two or three feet high and is sometimes wishfully called fish foam. But fish foam hasn't the density of suds, not at all, and smells like fish rather than perfume.

I mean, the river is a junkfest.

That's the Olentangy before it gets to campus, and before it passes the mysterious outflow pipes of a certain national research firm,[1] and arrives in the large-skyscraper downtown of

---

1. Home of at least some of the "Friends of the Olentangy," one of whom gave me a call after the first publication of this essay to invite me to plant trees along the river with his group. I said no, thinking it a conflict of at least my interest to get involved with the PR arm of such a large corporation.

Columbus. And Columbus is big—bigger than you might think, an Emerald City that pops up on the Central Ohio flats. It's said to be the biggest city in Ohio, population about 1.25 million inside the Greater Columbus loop of I-270. The city's official slogan should be IT'S NOT THAT BAD, since that's what people tell you, over and over. I think the actual civic slogan is MORE THAN YOU DREAMED. True. And that huge, worthy school where I had recently been tenured: 60,000 students, 15,000 staff, 5,000 faculty. Something like that. A city within the city. The Olentangy flows right through campus, unassaulted except by lawn chemicals and parking-lot runoff and frequent beer vomit on its way to the Scioto.

Columbus' two main rivers meet at Confluence Park. This is not really a park at all, but some kind of convention or catering facility on city land, probably the result of all kinds of inside deals. I took the dogs there once in my early search for dog-walking paradises. Confluence Park was hard to find. There are so many roads crisscrossing each other and exit ramps and overpasses that you pass the place ten times before you get to it, a scavenger hunt of signage, and then when you finally get there it's just another parking lot next to the river. Oh, and the catering facility and their big dumpsters overflowing with whatever party has just come through, making someone a nice private profit on public land, is my guess. And meanwhile, plentiful homeless have pulled all the liquor bottles out of the dumpsters for years, getting those last drops then creating a midden of broken glass down along the water.[2] No park at all, just a steep, rocky, trash-strewn embankment forming a point of land where our two protagonist rivers mightily meet, the greater silt carry of the Olentangy coloring the greater water volume of the Scioto somewhat. Here the Olentangy gives up its name, and the two are one: Scioto.

Which marriage flows through the big city under several bridges, looking like the Seine in Paris (the Seine a dead river,

---

2. I'm not making any cause-and-effect claim here, but in the months after the first publication of this essay, the embankment under the catering facility and the grounds immediately around it were cleaned up quite thoroughly, and have been attended to since.

by the way, fishless, oxygenless, killed, unlike the Scioto). But the Scioto is not a navigable river like the Seine; the Scioto's only four feet deep and heavily ensilted. I won't say much about the appealing replica of the Santa Maria that floats here trapped in a specially dredged corner under the Broad Street bridge in a 500th-year anniversary testament to a man who never reached the Midwest but gave his name to our fair city nevertheless.

Anyway, just below town, the river pillows over a containment dam a couple of hundred yards wide, a very pretty fall, really, the funny river smell coming up, men fishing, bums and bummettes and bumminas lounging, bike path twisting alongside, highway bridges, rail bridges, two turtles on a warm rock in spring, egrets, herons, seagulls, swans, busterns, kingfishers, beavers, muskrats, rats.

And no dearth of trees to catch the trash after flood! Maple, ash, cherry, gum, walnut, oak, locust, sycamore—on and on, dominated thoroughly by cottonwoods, which in the spring leave a blanket of cottony seed parachutes in a layer like snow.

The parks once you pass below the city are more than a little tawdry—poorly cared for, placed near the police impoundment lot and the railroad yards and light industry and a complicated series of unused cement ponds that once surely were meant as a sewage-treatment facility. Oh, and also in sight is the practice tower for the fire department, which trainers douse with kerosene and burn for the recruits to put out. Miles and miles of chain-link fence, altogether.

On the northeast bank of the river is Blowjob Park (one of my students called it in an aside in a paper), which I found because it is at the very end of the bike path. The path ends at a parking lot, where lonely and harmless-looking men sit in cars gazing at each other and waiting for liaisons. The city sometimes arrests these men in courageless raids, not a homophobic act, says a spokesperson, for the men are said not to be gay exactly, but married guys looking for action of any kind, loitering and littering and certainly dangerous so close to the impound lot and the defunct sewage-treatment plant.

When I moved downtown, downriver, to German Village (a turn-of-the-twentieth-century neighborhood—now trendy—

of brick dwellings and restaurants and shops, surrounded by what some Columbusites have called slums in warning me, but which are just further neighborhoods, with less and less money apparent, true, but plenty of lively children and sweet gardens and flashes of beauty in along with the ugliness, which isn't much worse than the general ugliness that pervades this end-of-the-eastern-woodlands city and its suburbs) . . . when I moved downtown, I brought the dogs over there for a walk and a swim, two of their favorite activities. Down below the dam, I nodded to men fishing, and the dogs raced happily, and it wasn't bad. You go down below the dam and the riverbank is broad and walkable in dry times—this first walk was in autumn—and you see good trees, remnants of the hardwood forest, and chunks of concrete under the Greenlawn Avenue bridge and rebar wire and yes, examples of all the junk listed above, particularly those plastic grocery bags in the trees, but fifty-five-gallon drums as well, and broke-down lawn chairs used for comfort by fishermen and abandoned when beyond hope. Also some real dumping—an exploded couch, perhaps thrown off the high bridge, and some kind of switchboard with wires dangling, and a filing cabinet with drawers labeled *Contracts*, *Abstracts*, *Accounts Payable*, and *Personnel*. It would not take much, I thought at the time, to figure out what local business all this came from. Might be fun to return it, but a lot of work. And probably they paid some asshole to cart the stuff to the dump, some asshole who kept the dump fee and emptied his truck off the Greenlawn Avenue bridge.

And down there, too, was a large concrete bastion of a culvert, labeled with a sign: *Caution, Combined Sewer Overflow*. In other words, when it rains, get out the way. And if you think "Combined Sewer Overflow" just means rainwater washed off parking lots, listen: in the rich, dried mud right exactly there, the dogs and I hiked through a thousand, no, *ten thousand*, plants I recognized (and you would recognize, too, at once) as tomato vines. How did so many tomato plants get sown? Well, tomato seeds don't readily digest, generally pass through the human digestive tract unscathed. You get the picture.

And the doggies and I walked that sweet fall day. After the bridge it's hard going, a rocky bank strewn with valueless trash, but also bedding and clothes, particularly male underwear for some reason. It's not too pleasant, and getting steep, so I turn back, but not before noting that across the river there is much parklike land, sandy soils under great canopy trees. Dog paradise. How to get there?

Wally and Desmond and I hike back to the car, drive clear around to the Greenlawn Avenue bridge (it looks very different from above), and find the entrance to what is called Berliner Park. I'm excited. There are baseball fields and a basketball dome and a paved bike path along the river (a discontinuous section, as it turns out, of the Olentangy bicycle trail that also passes through the Whetstone Park mentioned above), and many footpaths to the water.

In the woods along the river there is the familiar trash, of course, multiplied enormously by the location just below the city and just below the dam. Here's how it gets there: rain falls, perhaps during one of the many thunderstorms Columbus enjoys. The parking lots puddle, then begin to flow, carrying gasoline and oil and antifreeze of course, but also cigarette butts and cigarette packs and chaw containers and pop bottles and aerosol cans and many tires, just simply whatever is there. The light stuff gets to the river fast. Tires move a few feet per rainstorm, but they make their ways, oh, make their ways to the river or get stuck trying. Shopping carts probably have to be actually thrown in, but shopping bags get there two ways—flow and blow. Kids' toys are carried downstream just like anything else. And what can't float waits for a flood. Anything can ride a flood! Anything at all!

It's a mess. In fact, the part of Berliner Park that lies along the river is so bad that most people just won't hang out there. That leaves it open to what I call lurkers, men who lurk in the trees and know that my two dogs mean I'm a dog walker and not a lurker, and so not to approach. My dogs have even learned to ignore them, and I have, too. Each to his own.

Except for the one lunkhead who threw a rock in the path in front of my wife, but he seemed just developmentally delayed, no malice, and with the dogs along gentle Juliet felt safe enough, but hurried up out of his purview.

And except for the dead body I saw police divers pull out of a snag one day. Female, probably the suicide that had been reported two months earlier, although that jumper from the Greenlawn bridge had been identified as male by witnesses who tried to stop him jumping. The dogs rushed to have a look, came back quick. I talked to the cops a little. 'Nother day, 'nother dollar kind of talk.

And once I found a note—poignant and plaintive, a personal ad aimed directly at its market, pinned to a log: "Loking for love. Grate Sex. Call me up or meat heer, meet hear." Also this, written in Magic Marker on a bare-flayed log: SUCK YOU GOOD. With a shaky arrow pointing to an uninviting side path.

During one of our weekly phone talks, I told my mother about Berliner and all the trash. She said, Well, why don't you and a couple of your friends get together and go in there and clean it up?

She's right, of course. It's easy to complain and not do anything. But, Jesus, the flow of garbage is so great that my friends and I would need to work full time till retirement to keep up just with the one park. Perhaps the city could hire a River Keeper. I do pick up this bottle and that can, and fill a bag now and again. It's the least I can do. Yes, the least. Okay, I'm implicated here, too.

Downstream a little further there's another storm sewer–runoff warning, and the vile smell of unadulterated, uncomposted shit.[3] The bike path goes on. It's not a bad walk once you are past the stench, which takes a minute, because there is also a honey-truck dump station right there, which you can see from the path, a kind of long pit where the septic-tank-pumping trucks unload. This stuff has a more composted reek, a little less septic, so there's no danger of puking or anything. The dogs run on, free of their leashes, because there just isn't ever anybody around here, except lurkers. The dogs have no interest whatsoever in lurkers, and they love nothing more than a good stink. The path ends at a six-lane highway spur-and-exit com-

---

3. There's some kind of valve system here that's been replaced since the first publication of this essay. The new stuff looks pretty sophisticated, and the stench now is quite a bit less, yet still formidable, especially after rain. The pool in the river below stays thawed in winter, and ducks seem to like it.

plex, but not before passing a stump dump and a wrecking yard, ten thousand crashed cars or so in piles. Also a funny kind of graveyard for things of the city: highway signs, street-light poles, unused swimming rafts, traffic cones.[4] Under the highway bridge isn't too inviting, frightening in fact, but if you keep going there's a fire ring and much soggy bedding, a bum stop, and above you, up the bank and past a fence or two, the real city dump.

Here we (dogs, Juliet, myself) most commonly turn around and head back. And I guess I'd be hard-pressed to convince you or anyone that it's not that bad walking here. Really: it's not that bad. The dogs love it. But they do get burrs, and Wally, the big dope, insists on diving into the reeking storm sewer runoff, so we have to make him swim extra when we get upstream, where the water's cleaner. And note: the city's been working on the pump house. I mean, I'm not saying no one cares.

It's a nice place under the crap. The trees are still trees. And up in the trees the Carolina wrens are still Carolina wrens. And the wildflowers are still wildflowers even if they grow from an old chest of drawers. And the piles of stumps are pretty cool to look at. And the great mounds of concrete from demolition projects too, reminding me, actually, of Roman ruins, at least a little. And the sky is still the sky, and the river flows by below with the perfection of eddies and boils and riffles and pools. And the herons are still herons, and squawk. And the sound of the highway is not so different from the sound of the wind (except for the screeching and honking and sputtering). And the lights of the concrete plant are like sunset. And the train whistle is truly plaintive and romantic, and the buildings of the

---

4. And, come to think of it, a number of green-painted fifty-five-gallon drums, first about a dozen, then a few more each month or so, till there were over a hundred. You have to love the green paint, the purposeful co-optation of environmental-movement symbolism. These barrels disappeared just after the first publication of this essay, though again, I don't claim any connection. And one day I saw the "Neighborhood Outreach" truck from one of the huge local hospitals, an eighteen-wheeler, make its way into the chain-link compound and drop something—what exactly, I couldn't see from my vantage point, presumably some kind of outreach, though!

city a mile upstream are like cliffs, and I've heard that pere-grine falcons have been convinced to live there. And the earth is the earth, it is always the earth. And the sun is the sun, and shines. And the stars are the stars, and the sliver of the waxing moon appears in the evening, stench or no, and moves me. So don't think I'm saying it's all bad. It's not. I'm only saying that the bad part is *really* bad.

⁂

One fine blue day after much spring rain, Juliet and I in joy take the dogs down to Berliner Park, oh, early spring when the trees are still bare (but budded) and all the world is at its barest and ugliest, every flake of the forest floor unhidden, every fleck of litter and offal visible, and the turtles are not yet up from the mud.

We get out of the car next to a pile of litter someone has jettisoned (Burger King gets a nod here, and Marlboro), and walk down the dike through old magazines and condoms and smashed bottles to the dam to watch the high water of spring roaring over. In fact, the normal fifteen-foot plunge is now only two feet, and the water comes up clear to the platform where we normally stand high over the river to look, laps at our toes. There are percolating eddies and brown storms of water and the unbelievable force of all that liquid smoothly raging over the dam at several feet deep and twenty miles an hour. You would die fast in that river not because it is so very cold but be-cause of the super-complex and violent pattern of flow.

Juliet and I stare through the high chain-link and barbed-wire fence into the boiling maelstrom, absorb the roar wholly, lose our edges to the cool breezes flung up and the lucky charge all around us of negative ions as molecules are battered apart by this greatest force of nature: water unleashed. And so it's a moment before we see the flotsam trap, where an eddy returns anything that floats—anything—back to the dam and the blast of the falling river. And the falling river forms a clean foaming cut the length of the dam, a sharp line, a chasm; the river falls so hard and so fast that it drops under itself. And great logs are rolling at the juncture. And whole tree trunks, forty feet long, polished clean of bark and branches. And whole trees, a score or more, dive and roll and leap and disappear, then pop into the daylight like great whales sounding, float peacefully to the wall of water, which spins them lengthwise fast or sinks them instantly; and they disappear only to appear twenty feet downriver, sounding again, all but spouting, roaring up out of the water, ten, fifteen feet into the sky, only to fall back. Humpback whales, they are, sounding, rising, slapping and parting the water, floating purposefully again to the dam. It's an astonishing sight, objects so big under such thorough control and in such graceful movement, trees that in life only swayed and finally (a century or two of wind and bare winters) fell at river's edge.

And then I see the balls. At least five basketballs, and many softballs, and two soccer balls, and ten dark pink and stippled playground balls and forty littler balls of all colors and sizes, all of them bobbing up to the wall of water, rolling, then going under, accompanied by pop bottles of many hues and Styrofoam pieces and aerosol cans, polished. And a car tire with wheel, floating flat. This old roller hits the wall of water and bounces away slightly, floats back, bounces away, floats back, bounces away, floats back, is caught, disappears. Even the dogs love watching. They *love balls*, especially Wally, and are transfixed.

And the tire reappears long seconds after its immersion, appears many yards away, cresting like a dolphin. Logs pop out of the water like Titanic fishes, diving at the dam head-up the way salmon do (in fact, you see in the logs how salmon accomplish their feats: they use the power of the eddy, swim hard with the backcurrent, leap—even a log can do it!), leap among froth and playground balls and tires and bottles with caps on, balls and bottles and tires ajumble, reds and blues and yellows and pinks and purples and greens and blacks, bottles and aerosol cans and balls, balls and tires and logs and tree trunks and chunks of Styrofoam, all leaping and feinting and diving under and popping up and reappearing in colors not of the river: aquas and fuschias and metallics, WD-40 blue and Right Guard gold and polished wood and black of tire and crimson board and child's green ball and pummeled log and white seagulls hovering, darting for fish brought to the tortured surface in the chaos of trash and logs and toys, all of it bobbing, the logs diving headfirst at the dam, the balls rolling and popping free of the foam for airborne flights, and tires like dolphins, and soft-balls fired from the foam, and polished logs, and a babydoll body, all of it rumbling, caught in the dam wash for hours and days and nights of flood, rumbling and tumbling and popping free, rolling and diving and popping free, bubbling and plunging and popping free.

Sky Pond

In Maine, access to a swimming hole on a nice hidden lake or pond is not limited by any general law but only by NO TRESPASSING signs, generally placed on trees along roads one knows are near water by evidence of the quality of the sunlight and sometimes by cheerful stacks of little boards painted with family names and nailed on telephone poles, surmounted by the uncheerful and usually larger sign: PRIVATE. But even if there are no warnings, it's a hard heart that can walk right down some stranger's driveway to jump in a jewel Maine lake or pond.

The way in for the landlocked, then, is properly through the woods, crunch and snap down through the forest, picking a starting place where there are no driveways, dead reckon and battle your way downhill (it's always downhill, the last way to water, or something's amiss), hike till the water shines and flashes through the low branches of its trees, find your own little rock to sit on pondside, or, when the gods are with you, your own little beach at the lake. But that relies on a lot of luck and too much pluck for me most days—usually the spots where there are no driveways only persist in that agreeable condition because down at the water where a driveway would have led there is no proper shore, no place to build a camp, and most often the hiker ends up wrong side of a beaver bog or in the windward shallows, stiff breeze in the face, wading through muck and leeches thinking whether he can quite dive yet or needs to struggle further. Or you find that you've walked in behind the posting, nicely avoiding the signs (and so enjoying the woods) but not avoiding the trespass, and there's that big fellow raging over in his aluminum rowboat.

Anyway—Sky Pond had been like that for me. I'd crunched down through the woods—very steep grade—beaten my way down with my fly rod sometime during Juliet's and my first spring in the neighborhood (our house is three miles down-stream) and noted eight camps, one a derelict, the others but one empty off-season, the occupied one proud across the thick-est part of the pond high on a granite bluff behind stately pines. On the shore below that camp and on the boggier shore below its neighbor camp a total of three boats were turned turtle—a canoe and two rowboats. That day there was no breeze at all and the water was the sky and showed its own shoreline diving into the sky. So the poet named the pond.

I wanted a canoe. Here, by God, you'd do well in a canoe. Far off to the left you'd explore a cattail bog, far off to the right an alder bog. Well, *far* is only the word for the man on foot at the shores of a pond with no fisherman's paths around it (not so rare in Maine, where there are so many ponds and lakes). According to the Maine Atlas and Gazetteer map (a tall book of maps, which I'd left back up in the cab of my truck), Sky Pond is something slightly less than six-tenths of a mile long, two-tenths of a mile across at the widest point. I could swim to any point on its shore faster than I could walk.

As at most unbothered ponds, the trees at this northwest-ward shoreline were ancient and leaned out way over the water, all those decades of seeking light, leaned way out over their own tangled roots, these exposed by winter ice and the multicenten-nial splash of small waves. Under water in a pond like this, one sees "dead Indians," trees fallen in and preserved by the cold for centuries, all pointing to the deep center of the pond.

Trees, trees—gorgeous, but really there was no place to get a good cast, and the wading wasn't great. Yuck: a thick, rich, old humus bottom under twelve inches of water that neverthe-less put you up to your thighs immediately, so no way to get yourself properly out from under the leaners to fish. Still I tied on a black beetle imitation—just a spot of yellow on it—and pulled in sunfish one after the next, trying not to torture them, popping them off the barbless hook right at the water, not even bringing them quite to hand, enjoying this, and the smell of fish that got on my fingers, and the sharp pricks of their staunch dorsal fins and the wriggle of the little lives inside scales, the furious kicking caudal fin, the heat of life in their rolling eyes. There's also pleasure in the little mind game of knowing one wouldn't have starved had everything depended on the fishing.

The only places I could see around Sky Pond to cast were the cuts in front of the camps—and I'm just not the sort to stand in someone's yard, whether they are gone or no. Some roll casting got my beetle out to four or five little yellow perch. A nice afternoon of it. My first Sky Pond day and the last for a couple of years: other places I could get my canoe in more easily, here you'd have to trespass. So Sky Pond resisted me, enforced a natural privacy not entirely invented by its lucky landholders.

My next Sky trip was a few Junes hence, after I'd made the happy acquaintance of Bob Kimber, who is an outdoorsman and a spirited, sunny writer, also a translator and a Princeton Ph.D.—but never mind all that (things he wouldn't tell you right away anyway), he is Bob and always cheerful and funny, always with a project and a helping hand. He's got a full head of white hair and gray and keeps himself groomed and lives in work clothes a lot and barks with laughter at one's jokes and makes his own great jokes and stands a little wiry and not too tall, gestures when he talks, waves his beat-up hands. He's handsome, too.

This day he has invited me to help him rebuild a friend's simple dock on Sky Pond, their old one having partially sunk and rotted some after many good years of service. Hot day and Bob and I are up to our hips in the chilly waters of June, pulling the old floater free—it's simply built, just spruce boards nailed across two stout trunks of spruce—twelve feet out into the pond, simple as that, and our new design will imitate the old one, do for the next twenty years. We pull the old floater free from the chains that hold it (these nailed to roots, ubiquitous Sky Pond roots), then just scoot it along the bank like a submarine coming in for shore leave, just a periscope and deck showing, send it along a hundred feet or so where it parks itself under a leaner and will sink over years to join all the dead Indians sunk there, to be preserved like them by the cold.

That particular camp is toward the alder end of the pond, west side, and in June one saw the lily pads floating across the way in bright sun—frog-jump leaves still small, blooms still tight balls. And to the south one saw electric lines, which must follow a road, and the road must cross an outflow stream, that is, pass over a bridge, but the land falls away over there, falls below pond level, which means there is a dike of some sort, a long dam, one would guess, which means beaver work, millennial beaver work, Sky Pond a beaver impoundment, could be 10,000 years old, 20,000, I don't know. The Sky Pond outlet stream couldn't be very long—it must join the Temple Stream immediately, the Temple Stream which I knew well even then, better now—it flows hidden in its own cut behind the Kimbers' farmhouse not a mile downhill from here in the intervale, then two miles more flows through the pastures below my own, and some of what flows is Sky Pond waters.

Bob had already cut trees for the floats and we just splashed them in the pond using a Peavey pole (my first time—Bob is always teaching me new things, showing me new tools, generous man), Peavey pole and log hook, splash and float and guide, lined the floats up parallel and sawed spruce boards to four feet, nailed these one at a time across the two new floats and pretty soon had a dock to stand on and dive.

After that we took the right of the helpful to take a swim now and again off that dock, I and my wife, Juliet, Bob and his wife, Rita, she a Swiss expatriot with wry smile and undependable knees. I mention the knees only because it explains her caution and force with our overexuberant dogs—one playful tumble into Rita might pop every tendon in sight. And our boys were playful, all right, racing through the underbrush with the Kimbers' late Lucy, an elegant little dog, chaser of chickadees (our fellows lean to squirrels), black flags of hair, gone a little white at her snout, distinguished older lady, and a very cheerful swimmer, since gone to her reward. Our Wally is a big mutt, black and white, all chest, a mighty swimmer (the spaniel in him), always has to be in the lead (whimpers piteously if he gets behind), shoulders out of the water. Desmond, our smaller dog—half Border collie, half Boston terrier, very handsome despite the odds—Desi is a more desperate swimmer, sinking up to his ears, kicking those little paws, always aimed at the nearest way out but happy to swim nevertheless. The three dogs would gambol and growl and tumble all around Rita's knees till Wally and Lucy hit the water, Wally in the lead, of course, snapping water bugs, and off the two of them would swim while the people among us got down to swimsuits, then one by one leapt or dove or climbed down off of the new spruce boards into deliciously warm water (if the weather had been sunny) or startlingly cold (if it had been raining), and we'd stroke and paddle and kick and glide straight across to the lily pads, turn when the cords of the plant wrapped our feet like seaweed and brought the idea of sinking to mind, brought the long hair of Undines to mind, those malevolent water sprites of olden Europe who lured sailors, swimmers, drunkards to watery deaths through siren visions of beauty.

What lovely swims we had, the pond suddenly our own. We'd chat a little, our chins in lapping wavelets, then swim hard, an hour or so's outing at the onset of many fine evenings (I believe the Kimbers swam *every* evening; we only joined them occasionally). But then the folks who owned the house turned up, about August, and the dock wasn't ours anymore. Nor Sky Pond, suddenly. Well, there are plenty of places to swim in Maine in August.

One of the camps came up for sale. This availability not the kind of thing normal mortals hear about. But Kimber has his Olympian ear to the pulse of the town of Temple and an eye to the sky and certain mysterious soulful links to Sky Pond, and had long wanted his own bit of shoreline. So pretty soon I was lucky enough to be helping Bob finish building his own little dock down the hard slope from his camp, an older, hand-built cabin with chimney about to fall (it has done so since) and out-house tilted, lovely porch reaching out into the trees on stilts incompletely stoned-in for a basement beneath, a rustic place, complete with a couple of hundred yards of shoreline that includes one of the Sky Pond beaver lodges (at the mouth of a brook), west side of the pond, nor far from where I stood fishing those years before. Access is a long and finally steep twitch road, little used, two grassy lanes not for just any all-wheel-drive vehicle, in fact in Bob's vision for foot traffic only, and once in a while for his cat-tread tractor.

Bob has invited me down to help with the dock with his usual generosity. He won't need my help all that much, but knows the little help I'll give will earn me a lowered-guilt family ticket to come swimming summer evenings just this lovely trio of miles from home.

When I get to the camp, hammer in hand, the dock is about built already, spruce boards, once again, but on a standing frame, and with a ladder. Wally has preceded me and is already halfway across the pond, zigzagging after water skeeters and dragonflies, no competition for first place to distract him into straight lines. Desi greets Bob effusively. And Greg Kimber is there, too—didn't see him at first—home from his on-his-own adventures and up to his chest in the pond, holding boards for his dad. Of course, there's the usual father-and-son-doing-a-project-together tension in the air. I bark out jokes to make room for my presence. "Let me stand on your shoulders, there, Greg," stuff like that, not really funny at all, but funny enough.

And Greg wades up out of the water. He's built slender like Bob, his hair long, his head full of gardening knowledge and good dreams of communal living and community life. He's a serious young man but good-humored. One feels well observed by him, but never judged. The dock's about finished when we hear the first rumbles of thunder. The pond goes all dark, flat and smooth, then suddenly erupts in wind devils and then whitecaps. Boom and crack, the storm is upon us, first drops falling, pond leaping up to meet the sky.

"Let's get in the water," Greg says wryly.

We hustle up to the shack, a few seconds scrabbling up the hill, but we're soaked down by the time we're inside. Desi trembles, presses up against my leg, quavers and whimpers, pants grotesquely. Wally, oblivious, just likes being with everyone, wags his tail, looks for a hand to scratch his ears. The rain redoubles. The surface of the pond goes invisible—it's all rainfall—, only the big white pines exist out there anymore, and the rain, the rain, the rain crashing down, close lightning, boom again, and crack. Desi quakes. But it's energizing, the storm, pure gaiety. The porch roof, which is also the porch ceiling, begins to drip a little, then to actually leak, then to rain upon us.

"Roof is pretty good," Greg says.

Bob's thinking, already coming down the hill in his tread-tractor with a load of shingles and rolls of tar paper and two ladders and ropes and maybe someone to help.

After that good day, Juliet and I and the boys swim off Bob's dock and never have that feeling of being somewhere we shouldn't, somewhere someone else considers private, the feeling we've had elsewhere. We swim across Sky Pond nearly every day in summer, sometimes with the Kimbers, often not, dogs in the lead, Juliet next, I always following, swim across to sit on a big rock over there in the sun, get warm, return, the widest part of the pond, not quite a quarter mile, no lily pads, often a loon diving nearby then surfacing nearer, diving, surfacing farther, diving, surfacing unseen. Wally pursues for a time, but soon returns to dragonflies and water skeeters—he'll never, ever get near a loon.

And after the swim if the mosquitoes aren't too bad we just stand on Bob's dock and watch the water and maybe talk a little about the work of the day, what I've planted, what Juliet's painted, what Bob is writing, what Rita is translating, how the various gardens are doing, what books we're reading. It's a very sturdy peace and with the exercise a bright one, bringing mind and body together into one pure thing. Some evenings a beaver swims by a hundred feet out, close enough to inspect us, get a sense of us. He swims past slowly, as if nonchalant, but his head turns subtly, watching.

One evening when we are just Juliet and me and dogs, I chance to look up. High, high above us there are dark birds working insects. At first I think swallows—but these are not swallows. Too big, though it's hard to judge size against nothing but clouds. The white spots on the underwings are unique—I take note, then look in my bird book at home: nighthawks, bearded birds, not properly hawks but whippoorwill relatives, nighthawks wheeling, diving, my first sighting ever. Sky Pond gives one these gifts.

The walk back up the trail from the Kimbers' is always sweet and quiet. One looks for mushrooms in the edges of the trail, looks for warblers in the firs, for lady's slippers in the leaf mold, for newts in the wet spots, for squirrels to chase, finds them all, this paradise.

So Sky Pond had accepted me, but only as a guest. And even as the guest of someone so generous as the Kimbers, I felt like Odysseus on Circe's Island, or less exaltedly, Nick Carraway at Gatsby's, or less yet, the neighbor kid at the house with a pool, or worse, a servant invited to Cinderella's ball (not even the char girl herself!), or lower even, the bride's brother's buddy who happens to be in town, or lower yet, a temp worker at his desk among dot-com millionaires. Lowest of the low: a cowbird egg in a warbler's nest.

And you know, you don't want to bug your host, don't want to take advantage, don't want to be there every second, never give them a minute to themselves. The Kimbers, bless them, they had their own routine of swimming every late afternoon. So Juliet and the dogs and I swam elsewhere often—the Sandy River especially, sometimes further away: Long Pond, Porter Pond, Clearwater Lake. But Sky Pond had charms like no other: its calm, its containment, its leaning trees. And was close to home, as well. Juliet and I tried coming later than Bob and Rita might, but that gave us the feeling of *avoiding* them, which was not our plan at all, though it was awkward nevertheless to run into them unannounced. Awkward for us, anyway: Bob and Rita didn't seem to mind. Except maybe at times the rambunctious dogs, who can't check their ecstasy at seeing the Kimbers, who launch into sarabandes of delight, a barkanalia.

Wally particularly is in love with Bob, having stayed with them during a long trip Juliet and I once took, moons over him, wants to eat him up, climb in his pocket.

And it's always Wally in trouble. One of his worst transgressions was of a late summer's evening, air warm, sky already coming dark, when Bob spotted a large snapping turtle swimming under the dock. I saw it, too, and we pointed and exclaimed and Rita came to look but never did see the turtle because our interest in the water right there caught Wally's interest and he leaped in just where the turtle was. Oh, *Wally!* Rita said, genuinely pissed. She had wanted to see that turtle!

I felt like a cowbird chick. I was a cowbird, all right.

It's not that I dreamt of owning a Sky Pond camp—that was too much to ask—but I hatched this plan: access. I especially wanted to get down to the pond with my canoe and do a little fishing without imposing on the Kimbers in any way. I'd heard from several neighbors that the pond was stocked with brookies, and Bob had mentioned pickerel, too. And a morning of perch ain't bad either. No one mentioned bass, but I bet bass were in there, too. (Bass, as it turns out, are not.)

So what about the outlet brook that flowed down to the Temple Stream over the lip of the ancient beaver dam? What of that? On the way home from our next Sky Pond swim, I had a look, drove up the dirt road that passes by the end of the pond, that passes along the top of what amounts to a dike, a dike built primarily by *rodents*. I drove slowly. You couldn't see Sky Pond at all through the thick alder leaves, but the alders were growing just there precisely because water was near, growing there soaking their roots in boggy percolations. The outlet stream, though, flowed nicely, flowed mildly but visibly under a little steel deck bridge which was not much more than a long section laid across the stream's banks. I stopped on the bridge, looked down happily. The water was four feet below, but looked pretty inviting, wide as the canoe was long, deep enough to paddle, mildest current. Access.

Juliet was game. We'd take the next beautiful morning off from projects. And that morning came a couple days later, a Thursday in July. We made a lunch—nice sandwiches and carrots and chocolate cookies, jugs of water, packed that and two big old towels and our swimsuits and a picnic blanket in the wetbag, also lots of other stuff: fly rod, fishing vest, length of rope, notebook, paddles, life vests, bird book, binoculars (two pair), drawing pad, plenty of pens and pencils.

We had ourselves a perfect day, clouds at the horizon only, puffs of dreams unmoving. To Sky Pond! On our own terms! Skyward ho!

And off we went, leaving the dogs home, poor beasts. But they'd be havoc in the narrow stream, and havoc with lunch. I parked the old truckeroo in a spot that had been parked many times, a little turnout. And breathlessly (I'm always breathless at a new canoeing place—not sure why), *breathlessly* I pulled the canoe off the truck, flipped it onto my shoulders, tipped it up to see out a little. What I saw was Juliet, looking like a model in her thrift-store bell-bottoms and spangly top, her sassy new haircut sharp at her shoulders, all that blond thick hair flashing in the sun, game smile flashing, too, got the paddles and life vests while I carried the canoe on my head. "Nice hat," she said, old joke.

"Nice haircut," said I, no master of the comeback. I mean, her haircut was nice, why would I make fun?

At the bridge I just plunked the canoe (a Mad River Explorer, chunky, funky, well used), plunked it down off my shoulders with a bounce, slid it bow first into the Sky Pond outlet stream, one smooth motion till I had to let go and the little boat tipped sideways, splashed in on its edge, taking a large gulp of water over the gunwale. So haul it up by the bowline, tip it, drip it, drop it correctly, guy it up to the bridge lengthwise. And it just fit bank to bank, measuring the bridge and the outlet stream precisely: sixteen feet.

Juliet dropped the paddles into the boat, dropped the wetbag and the layers of other stuff, then considered how to climb in. This would be no mean trick, with the canoe floating wobbly under the bridge. She lay down on the steel decking, swung her long legs out over the void, waved her feet experimentally over the canoe, kicking, but reaching nothing. She swam her arms then and we laughed until it wasn't so funny, she kind of stuck there on the bridge with her legs waving, her chest and belly pushed into the steel decking uncomfortably. Finally she made her move, lowered herself a notch, kicked the gunwale, pushing the boat farther under the bridge and out from under her. I pulled the painter in the very nick of time as she dropped, she not realizing the boat was in motion under her, this perfectly timed, supremely lucky motion that brought the gunwale back under her foot, past her foot exactly as she dropped.

"Perfect," I said.

"Cake," Juliet said. She brushed at her bell-bottoms and at her spangly top as I turned the canoe upstream using that bowline, turned it upstream with some force to get it moving, hopped in myself as the boat headed pondwards, leapt in what would have been a perfect graceful motion if I hadn't missed the wicker seat trying to sit, missed so as to fall on my butt on the bottom of the canoe behind the seat, my legs arched *over* the seat, my head back on the stern board.

"Earthquake?" Juliet said.

"Just another new way to do things," I said.

"I'm hungry," Juliet said.

"We've got a nice lunch," I said. "Thanks to you."

"Stop here and eat? We could sit on the bridge."

She is funny. And we sort of laughed, but sort of it wasn't that funny, since it was noon already and I was hungry too, starting to get that impatient feeling you get around the undertrained wait staff at resort restaurants. But we were off in the perfect day, perfect hungry happiness knowing that the pond was not a hundred yards away, lunch imminent, then maybe a swim. We paddled. The alders all around the outlet stream were thick, much chewed and trimmed by beavers, dense and forbidding. You'd never get a canoe through that in a million years even though flat water stood around them, never get through there at all without the stream and its beavers having cut this right of way, having cut their own little permanent channel in what I gathered was a kind of sub-pond a degree of altitude lower than the main pond's surface. There must be a beaver dam ahead. And there must be another dam behind, the one forming this dead water, the actual main dam forming Sky Pond, which must be somewhere out of sight below the steel deck bridge just before a mild fall to the Temple Stream.

The channel made a small turn in the dense alders, and sure enough, we were coming up on a beaver buffer dam, freshly topped. Bob had recently complained of the pond's level being higher than normal, and here (along with recent rains) was why: the beavers had added about six inches of material to their secondary Sky Pond dam—it crossed the channel here and continued on, sinuously, as far as I could follow it through the alder thicket, the whole construction backing water very calmly, just quietly holding back the whole top six inches of Sky Pond (how many gallons would that be? How many pounds?!). I bumped the bow of the canoe and thus Juliet up to the dam works, but she just sat, staring ahead, nice strong shoulders from years of swimming, thinking about something so very important that she didn't notice we'd paused, didn't even notice the bump.

So I stared too, not to disturb her, admiring the dam some more, the flat surface of pond slightly higher than the water we floated on at present, this long present moment, these beaver sticks chewed and stripped and pale (and at that moment looking strangely delicious), these alders around us, this blue sky above, great white arks of cloud forming, Sky Pond ahead. After several hundred heartbeats, Juliet noticed we were stopped.

"Get on out?" I said.

"Not on your life," she said.

"Just climb up on that bigger log there."

She didn't so much as twitch a muscle toward the bigger log. "'Just climb up on that bigger log there,'" she said, quoting me precisely.

So I turned the whole boat, backed myself up to it, and precariously climbed out, one foot then the other on that bigger log. I didn't want to damage any of the beaver works, but wouldn't—they had placed this thick log of popple atop the masterworks here, and this bit of inspired engineering I found I could stand on, full weight, without influencing it in any way. From that perch I bent to grasp the gunwales of the trusty canoe, turned it till Juliet was right there beside me, took her hand, pulled her up and onto the log with me. There the two of us teetered, quickly hustling the canoe over the dam (much shallower on the upstream side), over the dam and into the higher water, like going through a lock from one world to the next.

Back into the boat, and onward.

But the channel is far less defined than it's been in its first hundred yards. In fact, now there are two distinct channels, one straight ahead (which peters), one hard left, to the west. We paddle on against the mild current, bearing ourselves ceaselessly into the sky.

The clouds, lovely, seem to be getting bigger, taller, grander, grayer. And suddenly a full-figured one blocks the sun. I'm chilled just as suddenly, feel my feet damp in the well of the canoe, and the chill walks up my legs.

But westward ho! Lunch awaits!

We paddle through the continuing maze of alders, north a ways, seeing glimpses of the pond, then a little east, then north again, then hard west. The false channels are so short we don't have to follow any. But the real channel has gotten shallow, and we're often scraping aquatic grasses, the water slower over them, pushing instead of paddling. Finally we're out of the alders and into the light of the pond—the pond!—oh, it's lovely, not twenty yards away if one could walk or fly. But the channel ends. Grass hummocks stand in our way like humped dwarfs. The water all around us is filled with grasses and thick with dead leaves.

Decision made, I say, "I'll pull us right to the pond and just dry off later."

And hook a leg over the gunwale, gingerly disembark, one foot on a hummock. The hummock flops sideways while my other foot forces the canoe away. I go into a split that can only be corrected by hopping awkwardly off the hummock and into the water, which is cold, too, and knee deep, then thigh deep suddenly, lapping my cutoff shorts. Juliet turns to see what all the commotion has been. "'Pull us right to the pond!'" she says, quoting me again.

I laugh and hold the gunwale and take a step, which brings me up on something submerged, back to knee deep. The pond is just there—just those twenty yards. I push the canoe over the grasses in water and get about ten feet further, step-ping carefully, perhaps walking the length of a huge old log, perhaps walking the spine of a sea monster—the leaves and muck are too thick for me to see my feet, though the leaves and muck are plain to see through the clear top layers of water. A tornado of silt emerges at each slow step. The sun comes out. "Let's eat on those rocks over there," says Juliet, pointing—a short paddle across the pond, nice rock next to the closest camp, the camp with the homemade roll-out dock in full hot sun—so inviting, so close. I step again, step right off my sea-monster log, sink thigh deep. Another difficult step, pushing the canoe and Juliet ahead of me, and it's just a little deeper, though the bottom looks the same—loose leaves, tornadoes of silt, a foot deep. But I'm sinking. Slowly, slowly, I'm in up to my belt. "I'm sinking here," I say.

Juliet looks back, says, "Hurry, then." She's kidding. I think I detect some concern in the changing lineaments of her face.

But I sink some more, up to the bottom edge of the photo of Big Bend National Park on my t-shirt. Juliet's wryish face gives way to an alarmed face. "Stop sinking," she commands. She doesn't want to have lunch alone.

I've got hold of the gunwale of the canoe, so I don't think I'll go under if it comes to it, but I can't pull myself out of the muck because my weight tips the boat too much. I'm up to my nipples. Calmly, or at least trying to speak calmly, I say, "Do you think you can pull the canoe up a little? Maybe paddle some or push with the paddle or something along those lines and get the stern over me?" If I can hook my arms over the point of the stern, I can pull up against the whole length of the canoe, and Juliet's weight. Her spangly shirt glints in the sun. She sticks her paddle in to test the depth, and it sinks in muck, too. And then she paddles, giving it a good go. In fact, she thrashes the pond surface, but the boat is hung up just enough on grasses that only pushing off the bottom is going to work. But there's no bottom. Now I'm up to my shoulders, and that's really enough. I grab the gunwale, say, "lean hard to starboard."

"What does starboard mean?" Juliet says calmly.

"Toward the pond," I say. "At least in this case."

"Your hair is going to be ruined," Juliet says. And if you've seen my hair you know that this is very funny. We start giggling as my scraggly ponytail goes in, too, and then my chin. I think of Ken Kesey's *Sometimes a Great Notion*, that unforgettable final scene in which the burly logger is trapped underwater by a whole tree trunk in a flood, caught under there but in contact with the living world, holding hands with his brother, who's helping him breathe through a reed, and our man is breathing through this reed and has every chance of survival (the flood-waters are receding), but he just can't stand it and he *laughs*, laughs and laughs and laughs till he runs out of air and drowns, right at his brother's feet, his poor brother unable to help him, laughing too.

But Juliet and I laugh because I'm up to my lips now and still sinking and Juliet's leaning and I'm pulling hard on the gunwale, tipping the boat hard my way despite Juliet, tipping the boat with my greater weight and really the weight of the bottom of the pond, which is the weight of the entire planet, and the boat's tipping and Juliet is leaning and I can feel my fake Tevas straining at their cheap straps and I can feel my shorts coming off, but pull myself mightily, glad my arms are strong, pull down on the canoe, Juliet leaning further yet, I pulling hard, drawing my knees up in the horrible muck, pull, grunt, pull, increments of nothingness as the planet lets me go, pulling, breathing, trying not to laugh anymore though Juliet is wracked with giggles, pull myself stinking chthonically, popping suddenly right up and into the boat on top of the wetbag, which sudden action prompts a sudden reaction: Juliet almost flops in, too. But she grabs the opposite gunwale and saves herself. Whoosh! I'm alive and only wet to the neck. I scrabble around and get back on my seat. "Your turn," I say.

I'm freezing.

"Lunch?" Juliet says.

We sit a long time, just looking at Sky Pond. It's right there, lapping the last ridge of hummocks and sticks and bog matter only fifteen yards from the bow of our boat, and surely there's a way to do it, but. But. But we're starving. There's an ancient, ancient stump off to port twenty feet. "We've got a hundred feet of line in the wetbag," I say. I point to the stump, thinking how somehow you might lasso it and use it to pull boat and all to a firmer bottom.

"No," Juliet says.

I retrieve my paddle from the well of the canoe, push on a hummock to starboard, free us from the grass trap, and we back away from our one chance to make Sky Pond our own. We paddle backwards a hundred feet or so till there's a false channel we can turn in, and we do turn, and head back the way we came, looking one more time at each small channel to be sure, but there is no path to Sky. So back over the beaver dam, locking down to the sub-pond level, then to the bridge, and climb out of the boat, onto the steel deck, nicely solid. Pulling the boat back up by the bowline I feel that my arms are sore. Both arms, some funny muscle used only for bog self-rescue, placed there by God for bog pulls only, just in case, and today I had to use 'em. Ow.

We get everything loaded and it's two o'clock before the cowbird chicks are unpacking a soggy lunch on the Kimbers' dock in shivering shade under growing clouds. And the sandwiches are very good, the carrots terrific. The chocolate cookies are the best ever made or conceived.

Last bite and the sun comes back long enough to dry the mud on my legs, long enough to warm me so I can strip and dive in.

Sky Pond!

My friend Wes McNair, poet and professor, a lovely man the height and shoe size of a basketball star, eyeglasses of a poet, eyes of a poet (basketball skills of a poet, too), all gentle intelligence, long hands, New England to the bone yet tender (he's full of hugs, our Wes, no frost there), tells me with some excitement that a camp is for sale on Sky Pond. From what he tells me, it's the one on the property adjacent to Kimbers', the only camp on the north end of the pond, the only one with southern exposure, the flag camp, we've called it, because the people there fly an American flag. Wally and Desi have made quick reconnaissance missions down there adjunct to our walks to Kimbers'. But we cowbirds—Juliet and I—we've only looked off the bluff where the leafy two-track driveways part in a Y.

Now Wes's wife, Diane, singer and librarian (though not at the same time, one hopes), vegetarian cook and gardener (these related), Yankee wisdom, Yankee clarity, Yankee skepticism (that's our Diane), but full of a kind of un-Yankee, fully generous, marvelously melodious laughter, Diane gets behind the project, and before you know it, it's done. There's been no realtor, no ads, the word of only one mouth: Bob's. A national bank won't cough up the money, but our lovely local savings bank (Farmington, Maine) doesn't hesitate, and the McNairs' camp mortgage is secured.

That first summer Juliet and I are in heaven—Sky Pond is a pond of friends, suddenly. We still visit the Kimbers' to swim, sometimes in their company, as often not. Our welcome at the McNairs' new camp seems equally large, but still, we don't want to wear it out, or wear the McNairs out, especially in these first months of their ownership.

Juliet's got news, too: she's pregnant with our first child. In July it's seven months, August eight, and we lumber down the hill to the camps. In the water Juliet is still a porpoise— swimming is her favorite pregnant exercise—she's buoyant and round, full of this girl who will be born in September. Backstroke and the belly is prominent, looms out of the water, shines in the sun, you can't believe how gorgeous. But still Juliet swims faster than I can, and stays in longer. No danger of her sinking. She wears her same old two-piece throughout the pregnancy, slings the bottom piece low under her enormous belly, something she's learned watching me dress all these beer-belly years (I'm shaped like a basketball *fan*, but the swimming should help).

The swimming, the swimming. The swimming is the same as ever in some ways—except that now you look over at the flag camp and see the people there and feel somewhat under their gaze then realize that the people there are . . . Wes and Di! It's only a matter of five or six swims before we decide to swim over to their dock to say hi, pull ourselves up to barking dogs (Annie, Charlie), let leap our own barking dogs from the water.

Wes comes down bearing camera and gets great shots—of Juliet and me side by side with Elysia inside Juliet, our two glistening bellies in sunshine, the sunshine of their dock, our first Sky Pond sunbathing, in sight of Kimbers' shady dock. And Di comes down in bathing suit and Wes strips down to his from his great height and you realize these dear friends have legs you've never seen in the decade you've known them and entire bodies. And even on the threshold of sixty human years these bodies are beautiful, and Diane gets a noodle and wraps it around her ample self and floats off, learning to swim, buoyant as hell ("My boobs are so big they *float*," she calls merrily). And Wes swims out into the pond saying how cold but stays in long, gets his exercise.

Then we cowbirds swim away, I first, slower and impatient, Juliet next, fast and full, Wally a gargantuan leap from the dock and passes me instantly and snaps bugs and gone off on his many missions: loons, water skeeters, drifting scents. Desi, though, Desi would just as soon not *leap* in but can't figure the best way to get closer to the water so he can be dainty about the thing. He barks and cries piteously, leaps from dock to canoe to dock and back again, not heeding Wes's advice ("Over here, over here, Desmond!"), not heeding Diane's ("Desi, you big dumb mammal, down here!"), but pacing and whining and finally not jumping at all but having a brainstorm, spin and run back off the dock, spin and run, *race* us barking back through the forest, no slow swimming for him, no contest. He has to wait a long while but meets us gaily at Kimbers' dock when we arrive. There we dress.

We come to the McNairs' by land, too, come and do jigsaw puzzles; we eat, we drink, we talk—it's a place to talk (Wes has said). We see the McNairs' visitors, get their talk, too. Sometimes the visitors are the Kimbers, and then it's a Sky Pond quorum. So good to have all these friends so close and on water.

And we swim—from Kimbers' to McNairs'. At McNairs', we pull up on the dock and Wes and Di come down and we drip and chat and grow chilly; we dive in then and swim away, four heads. We're pond people, very nearly. We come with my dad when he visits and we come with Juliet's folks when they do and one fall day we even sneak onto the porch when no one is home so Juliet can sit in a rocking chair to breastfeed Elysia Pearl, newly arrived. We come for dinner, and we come to see the new stove (Kimber has helped install it), and we come to see the weasel Annie has killed; we come just to be there. The evenings are best, as fall comes in and swimming is over for the year. One looks out over the pond and sees only sky (as Wes has pointed out), one sighs with the thought of winter.

One afternoon I pop over and it's just Wes and me and we talk and eat peanuts and drink small sips of whiskey and then beers. In the failing light Wes points out a particular camp down the way, the modest camp across from where Bob and I once built a dock together, the plain-hewn camp with rocks I often notice, with trees where the heron roosts, the camp with the homemade dock on rollers: "I haven't seen many people there this summer—not once this summer have I seen those people. It's an old guy. And his daughters are grown and gone off and have better things to do. You know that kind of thing. Kimber thinks they'll be wanting to sell soon."

I think of Elysia jumping from the old handmade dock into the sky down there. Think of all our heads bobbing through the water over to Kimbers', thence to McNairs', thence home again. Fire in the hearth, pot of soup in the fire, feet on the stool, book in the lap. Juliet making watercolors. No phone, no power, outhouse mildly fragrant. Elysia playing jacks with a friend out on the moss, five or nine or twelve years old. Kissing her boyfriend out on the moss. Just a vision, that's all. Not a premonition. Certainly doesn't mean I'm going to be able to buy any camp, not even that nice old one over there on Lucy Point (named by Bob after their late lovely pup). Not even that nice one over there under tallest white pines with dock not even rolled out this summer, not even once.

My Life as a Move

It's about geography, I keep telling myself. One has one's internal landscape painted by age forty or so. One's external landscape had better match. In Ohio, I kept looking for the sea, looking for ponds and lakes, looking for a recognizable kind of river, one that tumbles through rocks. I kept looking for a mountain, and mountains. The dirt, I thought, shouldn't be so white. The views should be longer. The clouds ought to be this way, the air should smell thus. And even after six partial years (Juliet and I never gave up Maine summers, and only three Maine autumns), even after all that time, I walked around feeling strange (as in *stranger*), an oddity, an outlander. It's geography and not just me, is what I say.

But it's easy to blame a place for every misery, and I think I did this in Ohio, sometimes getting mean about it, for example, making up state mottoes: *Ohio: Perfectly Acceptable!* But I liked a lot about Ohio (of which large place I know only Columbus very well). I liked the thunderstorms in spring, some lasting all day, all night, all of another day. I liked the possibility of tornadoes. I liked the caves in the Hocking Hills, and I liked the forests preserved there, the huge trees (especially the hemlocks), the tight hills and hollows, the scruffy farms. I liked the cornfields, the Amish buggies, the million hawks, the scarlet tanager, the flocks of ducks, the convocations of great blue herons. I liked very much being at the far west side of the

Eastern time zone, sunset nearly two hours later all year than in Maine, mornings dark. In the city I liked the museums. I liked the conservatory and its tropical rooms, its desert rooms, the bonsai trees. I liked the wonderful gardens everywhere around town, I liked the baseball games at all levels. I liked certain restaurants abjectly. I liked the trains, long freight and coal trains that rumbled in the night, romantic whistles, even a derailing crash or two in my short time there at the nexus of so many lines. I liked the Ohio State University campus, especially the oval and pond, designed by Frederick Law Olmstead when he was only twenty-three. I liked things about the abstract university, too, and things about my job there. And of course I liked many people, and miss them already, though some seemed so very odd to me, built of confidently Ohio pieces I didn't understand and couldn't quite guess at. The others came from other places, so at least were as tentative as I. When an easterner turned up in any of my classes, I knew it right away from something about the quality of the air around her, something ineffable but real.

Elysia was born in Maine in an autumn I was off duty from teaching and so released from Ohio. Holding her from the first minutes I knew what it felt like to be home, really home, and to leave seemed unthinkable. I wanted unequivocally to raise her in Maine. Because somehow that has become my landscape; that, somehow, is where I'm from, is where I am even when I'm not. I did not want to look at my daughter on, say, her tenth birthday, and think (as did a transplanted friend of his own daughter): *Oh my God, she's from Ohio.*

In the nights after my wife and our dogs and I moved into our nice-enough rented house in the German Village section of Columbus, Juliet couldn't figure out where to sleep. Moving in we had picked the smaller of the two bedrooms because it would be further from the quaint brick street and the all-night rattling of old cars and empty trucks and the intermittent rumbling of tires. But our neighbors to the north (a sweet and yet irascible couple whom we already miss) had a bright and necessary security light that shone in the windows of that back room like a flying-saucer transport ray that I could only wish would beam us up and elsewhere. And only a block away was High Street, the main drag of a whole city: sirens and laughter and fast-food order-up speakers turned up too loud in winter.

Welcome to Long John Silver's!

The problem wasn't urban-ness; we'd lived in plenty of cities, including New York, where Juliet grew up. The problem, perhaps, was this particular brand of urban-ness, these houses that filled old pastures for mile upon mile reached on roads that looked all the very same with the same mall repeated and repetitious fast-food signage and a thousand identical stop-lights at near-identical intersections timed slower than I was used to: one sat at the lights all day as various arrows came green, went orange, went red. The green light only released one to more of the same.

I'd wake in the middle of the night to Juliet clambering out of bed and tromping into the front room to lie on the guest futon in her nightie. Then I'd wake to her emphatic return. Then wake to her tossing again, then rising again, this time an-grily taking all the covers with her to the front room, accusingly leaving me there naked and horripilant on a bare sheet.

This went on at least a week. I'd say, "Sweetie?"

May I take your order?

And since I was awake anyway, she'd let me have it: Why did we have to move so much! She hated Columbus! She hated this house! She hated her new studio! She never wanted to move again! How did she get stuck in a life of following a *hus-band* around?! What about New York! What about Maine! What about *her* career? What about *that?*

What could I say? She was right. My job had brought us here, nothing else, unless it was ambition, my own. And my idea that Ohio wasn't permanent, repeated soothingly, was no comfort at all, none.

✑

About that time I heard a Tibetan Buddhist monk on public radio tell his famous host that indeed he was jetlagged after his trip, just waiting for his soul to catch up. That's all he said about that, kind of under his breath. But souls, I gathered, can go only at soul speed, faster than walking but slower than flying in a jet. Maybe about as fast as driving in a car around town, about thirty miles an hour, or forty. So of course you're going to feel weird after a fast trip of any kind. You drive four hours at sixty-five miles an hour and don't feel right till your soul gets there, about halfway through dinner.

And souls must travel at different rates. Certain politicians and businessmen seem to have very fast souls. Dog souls travel like dog shadows: full speed and not detachable. The evidence shows that my own soul is not only detachable, but is a dismally slow traveler. Juliet's, I think, slower yet.

And yet we've moved relatively a lot. From a one-bedroom on West 93rd Street in New York when we were married (June 1990) to Cerqueux-sous-Passavant, Maine-et-Loire, France (I count this as a move even though it was our honeymoon—those six weeks in the same converted farm building, the two of us working the whole time—because it was the beginning of the tearing from New York City and her family of my wife, and from youth of myself: brutal separation, intense transition, how else define a move?). Thence to my sister Carol's place in Helena, Montana (this in September, still 1990, in our used minivan weighed down to the wheel wells with far too many and mostly pathetic belongings, a huge pile of extra stuff wrapped in one of those blue tarps and tied to the roof—we took out a motel canopy in, oh my God, *Ohio*, had to stay a miserable extra day), just a few weeks on Carol's office floor on a guest mattress till Juliet and I found our own rather crummy place to rent on Rodney Street. We weren't perfectly happy there, but we had my sister's friends to hang with, a book contract in hand, a hospital job for Juliet, part-time. Midwinter I flew off to Maine to interview at the University of Maine at Farmington, got the job somehow.

So in August 1991, we were moving once again. We rented a U-Haul, loaded it full and loaded our new used vehicle (Juliet had had a terrible car wreck during our Christmas visit to Seattle, long story), loaded to the ceiling with even more belongings (and a new canoe on top), and drove five days east with Desmond, a puppy then, our souls plodding way, *way* after. I still miss the Rocky Mountains, the Missouri River, and a place called the Broadwater, a hot springs with two huge swimming pools you could paddle in at midnight, forty below in February, and watch the stars turn through pool mist.

We seem to grant to our high-speed roads and our airlines the rather thoughtless assumption that people can change places as rapidly as their bodies can be transported.

—Wendell Berry

Juliet's body, mind you, was being transported to a town she'd never seen. She fell into appropriate tears at our prospects daily in those first months: she was friendless, ungrounded, unmoored. She'd just been getting settled in Montana, and even though we'd never thought our tenure there would be permanent (unto death, I guess that means), leaving was all but *traumatic*. I was in the same straits, but *I had a job,* and those hundred instant contacts made all the difference. No amount of Maine beauty and no amount of saying I would have been glad to follow her somewhere and no amount of knowing that we were running out of money in Montana assuaged her, understandably.

The university is delicate about all this, with much discussion of spousal advocacy and spousal hiring (much discussion, little action). But corporate America and sociologists (like Anne B. Hendershott, in her book *Moving for Work*) call women who thusly follow their husbands "trailing wives," as if this were a neutral term. *Trailing wives!*

Therapists write little books of self-help for the move, talk about moving as if it were death followed by grieving, in Kübler-Ross stages: denial (refusal to pack), anger (you patriarchal *motherfucker,* why do we have to move!), depression (I hate this place, I'm tired, I don't want to see anyone), bargaining (next time we move for *me!*). The final stage is acceptance. Poor, trailing Juliet got through the first four stages pretty quickly in Ohio. The fifth, acceptance, she never found, in fact, had her own name for it: "Stepford Wives." *Oh, honey, really, it's so lovely here. I just want to thank you and your job for everything.*

Me, I never got past anger, maybe stuck there since I was six years old. But more about that shortly.

✒

Our first house in Maine was a rental, and it's possible our souls never lived in that good house at all, so slow was their trek eastward from Montana. After a year in Maine, though, we bought this place (our first!), ten miles further upstream along the lovely Sandy River from our original landing place and moved yet again, making many trips with the help of many new acquaintances in many old pickup trucks, the two of us now thoroughly saddled with belongings. We worked on our house for four years, really enjoying the nesting, the owning, the improving, the sense of continuity, of place. Juliet started and built an independent art therapy practice, making use of her Pratt Institute degree (Master of Psychological Studies) and unbelievable entrepreneurial pluck. I taught. For the health of her soul, Juliet painted, grew into her talent. For the health of my soul, I puttered in the garden, grew into the dirt.

We hiked in the woods. We swam in the rivers and ponds and lakes. We skied and skated and shoveled snow. Juliet said she had never been so happy. We were in love with our house, smitten. We were in love with our town. We got a new dog, a pal for jealous Desmond. We had enough money for the first time ever. Life was good.

If it were all about geography, we'd have simply stayed put.

But after only four years (it seems longer than that now), after only *four years*, the length of, say, a college career, our settled bliss began to ripple, then quake, finally blew up. My job, with its heavy load (teaching the least and best of it—I'm not a bad teacher, dedicated to the point of exhaustion, grumpy but well-meaning, focused on my students' independence so fiercely that they often think I'm abandoning them, which I am, in a benign kind of way), the *job* had got in the way of my writing and reading, and in truth of teaching itself. All along, I had to admit, I'd had my academic sights set higher. And my real sights were set on . . . *getting out*. Hard to admit (or even know, when the immediate pressing goal was tenure), but for me the university was only a contingency till writing might pay the way. And in the meantime, I needed a job that gave me time to *write*. Time to write my way out of academia altogether.

In the meantime, too, imperatives of career pulled at the geographical imperative. Temptation came along in the form of a writer acquaintance who insistently recruited me for Ohio State (of all places), came during a particularly sharp but now forgettable battle with administrators over my promised early promotion. I won and was promoted because I was willing to leave, and I was willing to leave because the battle had come about at all. With a job change and move I could free myself from pettiness, punish my tormentors, so I thought. Still, I wouldn't have considered the offer from Ohio State if Juliet had not decided at just that time to go for an M.F.A. in painting. This M.F.A. could not be postponed any longer. She sent out applications to all the best schools. The times, they were a-changing.

Geography, what is it? Just a backdrop to career. A coincidence of career. I lay in bed wondering how I could ever leave our little house. All the work we'd done! And somehow, at forty-some, roots had grown from my feet and found the earth. I felt deeply dug in, thoroughly connected. But this new job was big time, I told myself. I'd have *grad students*. I'd have a raise of nearly *one hundred percent*, over time. I'd *halve* my teaching load. I'd write and write, and write myself right out of there. But Maine!

Geography, gravity on its side, was winning. The decision was all but made: we'd stay. UMF would promote me, give me a competitive raise. But then Juliet was accepted into the painting program at the School of the Art Institute of Chicago. That tipped the balance. I took the job at Ohio State. Still unsure, I asked for a leave of absence from UMF, and was kindly obliged: two years.

Ambition cared little about continuity or place or friendships or the travel weariness of souls or the five stages of grieving. Ambition looks up into the clouds and likes what it thinks it sees up there, doesn't care at all about the rugged or impassable or even deadly cliffs and gorges and precipices its owner must stagger through and climb over on his way (hers, too) to wherever, just as long as the direction looks like up.

The summer of 1995 was like this: drive to Chicago to look for and find an apartment for Juliet (there were lots of small apartments available, because, horribly, the heat had killed hundreds of old people that summer), then to Columbus to find an apartment for me. Motels and hotels and weeks of bad food. Then back to Maine (ah, sweet and cool Maine, where no one dies of the heat, but maybe of hitting a moose with a car!) to pack, and to consider the incredible range of response from friends to our leaving (veiled anger mostly, at perceived abandonment), then back to Chicago to move Juliet into her new digs (an apartment so small that perhaps I should call it a dig), then to Columbus to move me into mine (a pleasingly eccentric sublet from people who have since become good friends). Despite the stresses of all this we did one smart thing, at least: we kept our house in Maine. It's cheap enough (our fifteen-year mortgage, now two-thirds paid, is $369.12 a month), and to sell it would have been to cut our anchor chain in a storm.

We sped a thousand miles back to Maine that first June in the Year of Ambition, but Juliet lived nine weeks of that summer, day and night, at the Skowhegan School of Art, where she'd won a prestigious fellowship. At Juliet's soul speed—in, say, a canoe—the town of Skowhegan would be something like thirty hours from our nest, downstream along the Temple Stream to the Sandy River to the Kennebec River. By car on good roads it's only forty-five minutes, but forty-five minutes made all the difference for Jules that summer; she was away from home and from me no matter how close. We had two weeks together unrelaxed before September came and the long drives back to our separate cities. Then back to Maine in June, Juliet with a School of the Art Institute of Chicago painting degree in hand, then September, and back both of us to one city, Columbus, German Village, to that weary military-surplus-brown rental house where

Juliet couldn't figure out what room to sleep in, that Ohio town full of Ohio people, that outpost on the edges of the ancient prairie, at the ends of the eastern forest, through winter, through seductive early spring. Then back to Maine, and forth to Ohio, and back, a rhythm our hearts began to understand, if not our souls: moving, moving, all the time *moving*, tolerated till the baby came. Elysia slept in my arms and made me see that my soul had never left the house in Maine, not even to look down the street and see where the rest of me had gone.

✐

Here is more from *Moving for Work*, by our favorite sociologist, Anne B. Hendershott. It's actually a footnote to the following rather familiar sentence: "On the list of all time stressful events, moving comes right after the death or divorce of a spouse." Familiar sentence, because Juliet and I kept repeating it to each other as we moved, possibly as an explanation for why we felt so grouchy, but possibly as a threat. The footnote:

Change in living conditions carries 20 "stressor points" according to *The Social Readjustment Rating Scale* by T.H. Holmes and R.H. Rahe published in the *Journal of Psychosomatic Research* 11 (1967): 213–218. However, while 20 points in itself would not be difficult to manage, a move for work carries an additional 36 stressor points, a change in financial state (positive or negative) carries an additional 38 stressor points, a new mortgage carries 31 stressor points, a change in responsibilities at work carries another 29 stressor points, having a spouse begin or stop work brings another 26 stressor points, and a change in recreation brings 19 points, a change in church activities brings another 19 points, and the 18 points that a change in social activities causes brings the total number of stressor points caused by moving to an alarming 236 stressor points. In contrast, the death of a spouse carries 100 points in itself, and divorce carries 73 points.

I'll let my reader argue with Dr. Hendershott about stressor points (don't death and divorce lead to changes as harrowing as and much worse than those of moving?), and merely point out that at least Juliet and I didn't have church activities to make things worse.

$\mathscr{D}$

I was born inside St. Luke's Hospital in Chicago, August 18, 1953. We—my mother, father, older brother and I—lived in Park Forest, near the big city, till I was but one year of age, at which time I was moved to Needham, Massachusetts, where my memory dawns (though in an inkling way I remember some vague something about my street in Park Forest). Did that move cast the psychic mold for my later life of constant moves and upsetting dis-ubiety?

The house in Needham was brown, as was the family station wagon. My dad was being promoted at work, and promotions meant hierarchical moves: Chicago office, Boston office, New York office.

The summer I turned tender six—that age when most psychologists agree that identity and personality become firmly set—we (big brother Randy, Boston-born sister Carol, Mom, Dad, I) moved to New Canaan, Connecticut, a commuter exurb of New York City, one of those towns to which the golden honey of the big city flows, leaving the worker bees behind. The date was around August 20th, 1959, which I recall and can confirm easily because my little brother Douglas was being born. Thirty-three years later I would hold his new baby girl, dark and brown-eyed as he is, and like an explosion remember *holding him*, not déjà vu, not some kind of synaptic glitch, but *memory*, this little pink-brown baby in my arms. Memory full of emotion: love, jealousy, anger, curiosity. Memory full of the smells of that time, and of the feeling of displacement. I held Dougie's daughter and felt the old displacement again.

Imagine: my mother, already mother of three, already an uprooted (and perfectly nice) Midwesterner, gives birth in Boston, rests a day or two, and moves with new son to new town with no friends and husband under major-league pressure in a new office (he must have been stressed, Dad must, though he'd never say so; such was his training as a man), this husband away from home at least ten hours a day, an hour each way on the train to town, not to mention his frequent European and Asian and South American and African business trips of up to six weeks. Mom essentially alone in a new town, no relatives around, not even in-laws, no one at all, nothing, the phone thought of as too expensive except for emergency, and emotions no emergency. And how many additional "stressor points" should we award her for giving birth? For having four kids? For having *us* four kids? Then a fifth?

I was alone a great deal, my athlete big brother having hooked up with the sportsy kids in the neighborhood immediately upon our arrival and able to fend for himself (interestingly, he hasn't moved at all—still lives in New Canaan, not two miles from my parents' house). But even he came home—according to my mother, who remembers the scene to this day—came home after an altercation in the neighborhood and said "I don't even *like* it here," which made Mom cry.

I fished and roamed around in the woods contentedly alone, attached myself to the blue sky and turtles and ponds and large stumps and abandoned farm implements and mossy toadstool worlds the way I still do. There weren't any kids I liked around. I got pounded for being new, mostly, though Mike Vitello across the street invited me over to his house after punching me and throwing me in the gravel-pit pond, and we did hang out.

I started first grade in Center School because West School wasn't quite finished, so every kid from my part of town was moved at Christmastime to a new school building and huge raw playground where I broke Rosie Smith's glasses (maybe on purpose: a rock was involved, the glasses perhaps snatched from her face, perhaps by me) and some other girl's leg (absolutely by accident in a perfectly standard game of dodgeball, though I was thought guilty of violence after Rosie's glasses—so my parents were called in) and supposedly pushed Dale Lybrand down trying to kiss her, hurting her knee (though what I—really, truly—believe actually happened was that she fell chasing me in a game of stolen kisses, in which boys, and certainly I, always played the role of terrified prey). I got in trouble in other ways, too. Clearly I was pissed about something, and letting it be known. The move? The displacement? The trickle-down effects of the isolation of my mother, that trailing wife trailing kids?

When I was ten we moved to another house in New Canaan, a compact builder's cape with six bedrooms and four baths on an acre of ridge above a bird sanctuary. And I lived in that house (except for a few high-school summer months in Montana in the care of my Uncle Bill—my first fly-fishing, first extended backpacking, first times mostly naked with a girl I loved) until I went to college, and in that house my parents still live, same phone number since 1959. At least there is that phone number for continuity. At least my parents are still home when I call, knock wood.

The United States, let's face it, is a country of exiles. Not even the descendents of the original inhabitants live where they want to live, or where their people started out (in fact, most Native American tribes in the best of times moved camp several times a year following game or the weather; even agricultural tribes are said to have moved on when the soil got thin, two or three years of stasis at best; and all this moving must reflect the heritage of all humans, which must point to moving as an activity thoroughly atavistic and perfectly in character—so why am I moaning?). My parents, whose parents in turn were from elsewhere, both grew up in Liberty, Missouri, met when Dad came from another part of Kansas City in the seventh grade. They began going steady in high school and married at age nineteen. By the time they were thirty-six they'd moved step-by-step away from staunch Liberty and its Depression Victorianism to polished New Canaan and its permissive postwar optimism. Surely they were reeling, even if they were growing rich.

Part of the attraction of Maine for me, I think, is its strong resemblance to the Connecticut of my childhood (or at least the

Connecticut of my childhood perception) and therefore my memory. I didn't notice the wealth, particularly (not much of that in our part of present-day Maine). I didn't notice the separation of work and worker in the commuter ethos of our town. What I noticed as a kid was the forest, the ponds, the bogs, the many bugs, the bright and clear days, the distance to neighbors, the working farms, the old fellows in wool caps, the New England churches, the crocuses, the five hundred birds of summer, the bright leaves of fall in particular progression, the snow.

⌒

By my most conservative count I moved twenty-one times during my college years, from dorm to dorm, from farmhouse to farmhouse (and from band to band—I played piano), from shack-ups with more and less magnificent girlfriends to crowd scenes with student or musician roommates, from high above Cayuga's waters in the hills around Ithaca to a series of rundown houses on that deep and narrow lake, from protofamily to protofamily, some all brothers, some all sisters, several households mixed girls and boys (these the most comfortable and comforting to me), some of the band households mixed ages, as well. Unconsciously I was recreating the large group and the muted chaos that was my family. In those five years I lived with some *seventy-five* people in all. Not many are still on my radar screen today, but I'd gladly hug any one of them on sight. Maybe ten are still friends, though of those ten I regularly talk to only two or three or four. Several are dead—scary to say I can't say how many, except as a minimum: three.

Perhaps in all this moving around and confusion of allegiances and de-bonding and re-bonding I was recreating an insecurity that felt homey to me—not only emotional insecurity, but an insecure sense of place and belonging. Moving provided insecure circumstances I could then blame for any soul turmoil I felt instead of blaming the turmoil itself, this turmoil that has its roots in the early moves of my life and the effect of those moves on my parents. Moving! It's moving what made me bad!

Or maybe there was nothing for it; maybe if I wanted work and a life in the last part of the American Twentieth Century, *I had to be on the move.*

℘

From the time I finished college in 1976 (a year and three months late, the August I turned twenty-three) until the time I was married (at age thirty-six), I moved twenty-five more times, that is, completely relocated myself and my belongings to new parts of town or the country or the world, though some of these moves were toggle moves back and forth from New York City, where I'd established an agreeable home base and a rhythm of overwintering labor in the city and recreational estivation in the hills and shores. I had portable work: music, bartending, handyman, writing. From one house to another in Ithaca and surrounding towns six times, then to Seattle, two houses, then to Madison, Connecticut (while beloved Susan, who would have been my first wife in a different era, worked on her doctorate in music at Yale), then to Martha's Vineyard (escaping the *ménage* and suburbia and regaining a huge and roiling family of roommates), then to New York City for the first time, then back and forth, first from a loft in Soho, then a loft in the meat district west of the West Village, then the Upper-Upper West Side, to these places: Oslo, Norway; Lenox, Massachusetts; Meredith, Colorado; Helena, Montana; Dearborn, Montana; and Martha's Vineyard, Commonwealth of Massachusetts, all of them glorious places where a confirmed putterer could spend all his scraped-up money on the cheapest possible rents and on piles of used books and on ten million bottles of beer in the summery bosom of nature.

℘

An old teacher of Juliet's (along, I believe, with the counselors of AA) called it the geographic cure: you move to start a new life in a new place—erase the blackboard—only to discover that when the dust settles you're still you, with all your troubles intact, no matter that the street names are different, the second-tier fast food unfamiliar. The marks on the new slate as they appear despite you are in eerily the same handwriting.

A Zen saying puts it more cheerfully: Wherever you go, there you are.

And, of course, where you end up is everything in a move. In Montana, I felt my mind spreading out to fill the vast spaces around us. There I was. You could look off miles in every direction, and the sky was famously huge. Great valleys reached (and reach) miles to great ridges of mountains. It's all high and dry and always there's a wind. Newly wed, Juliet and I struggled to make friends—these Montana people were self-selected for the wide-open spaces, and they liked a lot of space around them, needed it. If you stood on the street to talk, your interlocutor stood four feet away. If you stepped a little closer, New York distance, two feet or so, your Montana acquaintance moved back to keep that wide valley between the mountain ranges that were your very separate selves. Always I felt I was hallooing across huge windswept geographical basins to have a conversation. Emotional space mimicked physical space—a visit once a month or so was considered a great deal of contact by our new friends. And their inner lives as you got to know them resembled the Great Plains, too: wide open spaces, inaccessible features. Hours of driving and the mountains no closer.

The plain, sturdy landscape of the central part of Ohio seems to attract plain, sturdy minds, smart people whose thoughts despite intelligence don't climb many hills, but hop on the perfectly straight interstate and go where they're going, whose rivers of emotion are stable, easily dammed, slow flowing, often muddy and brown, oxbows of indirection hiding great fish of aggression (I'm more of a grizzly bear— bite your goddamn head off, but at least you hear me coming), who like gatherings, since gathering is easy: high school football games in great stadiums, endless malls, giant universities. People who need dramatic or intricate or undulating or featured or obfuscatory landscape just don't stay here. People who don't, do. And they have children over generations so that a new species emerges: Ohio Man. Or am I just being mean, blaming Ohio and everyone living there for my own psychic struggles?

Hell, no!

And what about climate? In Ithaca, rain. And more rain. And snow. And more snow. Gray, gray, gray. That crazy town is equipped with gorges (you've seen the bumper sticker: "Ithaca is Gorges"), gorges to leap into when the gray skies get a person down. And people did leap. What sort of soul handles all that gray weather, all that rain, cheerfully?

Inner climate can be predicted from outer. Maine is full of chilly characters, forty degrees below zero on the warmth meter, perpetually sure the good news is about to turn bad. On the most perfect day of summer, say "Nice day" to a true Yankee and he'll say: "Winter is coming soon."

In Norway, there's the national jollity, which is the flip side of the national depression (c.f. Edvard Munch), which two poles form a picture of the year there: midnight sun at summer solstice, twenty-two hours of night at winter.

Thus does the geographical character of a place account for migration. It's no mistake or mystery that Scandinavians ended up in Minnesota. Maine surely reminded various strains of Brits of their beloved British Isles and French Canadians of their beloved French Canada. In Maine, at any rate, among the Smiths and the Butlers and the Porters and the Kings, the Castonguays and Beauvoirs and Bellefontaines and Roys, my last name is a constant source of conversation—the spelling is so mysterious, that crazy "h" on the end that sounds like a "k," wicked strange! One of my UMF students trying to remember my name to one of my distinguished colleagues said, "Oh, you know, that *foreigner*."

In Ohio, the immigration was largely German. No one there had the slightest trouble with my name (except that Nederlanish double "o"). But in Ohio people had trouble picking out who I was from the clues I gave: long hair, mustache, little beard (an imperial, or soul patch), beer belly: I'm read as a redneck or hillbilly. In Maine, I'm obviously a crunchie, which is a hippie (the etymology of the term having to do with granola). In New York, I might be taken for a construction worker, which is often what I was there. In Norway (during my brief tenure in Oslo playing music), I was taken for an American. In Paris, speaking French, I was taken for Norwegian. One loses sight of one's identity, place to place.

There you are, but different.

_🖋_

All these pages to say: I quit my job at Ohio State. Gave up tenure, gave up perks, gave up probably the best creative writing job in America. But Juliet and Elysia and the fellows and I are home. Home in Maine. And here, yes, we are recalling how cold the winters, how far the museums (but also how close New York, and Boston, and Montréal). We are home, we are home. Home in the bosom of friendships, among people who need to know the sea is near, who must climb a hill, dive in a pond, eat blueberries by the fistful.

These are peculiar thoughts: that it's one's parents who decide where one is from; that Juliet and I will be the ones to say where Elysia is from. And funnier yet to realize (Juliet and I looking at each other across the dinner table after a good visit to old home New York City) this: we may have _more_ moves in us, may really _need_ a city pole, may need a year in Europe, may need a break in winter. But the kid will have to go to school. And her parents will have in some degree to take advice from the grounded among us, from Scott Russell Sanders, for example, who says: _Stay put._

My hammock in Maine. I swing in a gentle breeze that smells of the ocean, that smells of the White Mountains. It's air I've known a long, long time, a place that feels right. Just there, Mount Blue. Familiar clouds, building higher. Over here my garden. The house with its thousand projects, right there. My new study in the sugar house, Juliet's new studio downtown, both of us having moved to make room for Elysia. Our kid. Our junk-filled sheds. Our woods. Our stream. Our many paths. Our many friends. Maybe we'll stay. Maybe we will.

Are we home?

Acknowledgments

Thanks to teachers: Philip Lopate, who got me writing essays in the first place; Frank McShane, who nudged me toward journalism; Joyce Johnson, who made me understand that memory approached honestly can aspire to art. Thanks to editors who are friends: Colin Harrison and Barbara Hanrahan especially. Betsy Lerner, too, my agent and old pal. And thanks to other friends—a list I better not even try to start—thank you all, especially those who find themselves snapshots in this album. (And thanks to the reader for forbearance: I've changed some names and some distinguishing characteristics to protect the privacy of certain people pictured here.) Thanks to the MacDowell Colony, heaven on earth. A special thanks to Maureen Stanton, who read many of these essays in draft and gave cheerful, smart encouragement just when I needed it. Thanks to Kristen, Beth, Rosalie, Madeline, Olivia, Isabella, Florin, and John, for endless inspiration. Thanks to Desmond and Wallace. And most of all, and always, thanks to Juliet, and now Elysia. *Lentior.*

INTO WOODS

was composed in 10.3/13 New Aster
on a Macintosh G4 using QuarkXPress 4.1
at Coghill Composition Company;
printed by sheet-fed offset
on 60# Arbor Smooth stock
(an acid-free paper) using soy-based ink,
smyth sewn over binder's boards
in Skivertex cloth with Permalin Colors endsheets,
and wrapped with dust jackets printed in four colors
on 80# enamel stock finished with film lamination
by Edwards Brothers, Inc.;
designed by Wendy McMillen;
published by
THE UNIVERSITY OF NOTRE DAME PRESS
Notre Dame, Indiana 46556